FVON I

Trailblazing
Georgians

Dedicated to history teachers everywhere, and in particular to Kathleen Le Mare of Frensham Heights School, who inspired a 10-year-old to have a dream which has lasted a lifetime.

Trailblazing
Georgians

The Unsung Men Who Helped
Shape the Modern World

Mike Rendell

PEN & SWORD
HISTORY

AN IMPRINT OF PEN & SWORD BOOKS LTD.
YORKSHIRE – PHILADELPHIA

First published in Great Britain in 2020 by
Pen & Sword History
An imprint of
Pen & Sword Books Ltd
Yorkshire - Philadelphia

Copyright © Mike Rendell, 2020

ISBN 978 1 47388 609 4

Typeset by Aura Technology and Software Services, India
Printed and bound in England By TJ International Ltd.

Pen & Sword Books Ltd incorporates the Imprints of Pen & Sword Books
Archaeology, Atlas, Aviation, Battleground, Discovery, Family History, History,
Maritime, Military, Naval, Politics, Railways, Select, Transport, True Crime,
Fiction, Frontline Books, Leo Cooper, Praetorian Press, Seaforth Publishing,
Wharncliffe and White Owl.

For a complete list of Pen & Sword titles please contact

PEN & SWORD BOOKS LIMITED
47 Church Street, Barnsley, South Yorkshire, S70 2AS, England
E-mail: enquiries@pen-and-sword.co.uk
Website: www.pen-and-sword.co.uk

or

PEN AND SWORD BOOKS
1950 Lawrence Rd, Havertown, PA 19083, USA
E-mail: uspen-and-sword@casematepublishers.com
Website: www.penandswordbooks.com

Contents

Preface

In one of my previous books, *Trailblazing Women of the Georgian Era*, I looked at some of the women who 'broke the mould' – who dared to succeed in what was very much a man's world. Women were the disenfranchised minority – an underclass denied education and legal rights. Yet some stood out and challenged the perception that women were only fit for running the home and rearing the nation's children. I felt that such pioneers deserved to be remembered.

In this book I want to look at a different section of under-appreciated people, coming from a very different group. For a start, they are all men. They were not downtrodden or denied opportunity – but for one reason or another they have never received the recognition they deserve.

Their story plays on the age-old question: what is fame? Nowadays, we live in an era where, as Andy Warhol said, we all get our fifteen minutes of fame. Some get rather more than their allotted quarter of an hour – think of the people 'famous for being famous' – such as the Kim Kardashians of the world. Think of all the Z list 'celebrities' who strut their stuff on reality TV shows – for them fame is something they strive for as an end in itself. They have no aspiration to change the world, no lifetime of service or devoted care to others, no intention of easing suffering in the sick or disadvantaged, or giving the world some life-enhancing invention. For them, they seek only to fuel the need of our modern world to raise ordinary people to a celebrity status. No matter to them that time will probably knock them down, or that future generations will wonder what all the fuss was about.

I would prefer to look at fame as something earned, out of respect for effort and achievement – and there are some interesting examples from the eighteenth century which show how transient and capricious fame could be. Think of Philip Astley – nowadays, hardly a household name, but in his day he was described as having the second-best known face in the whole country. Second? Yes, because the face of the king was the best known, largely on account of the fact that the bust of George III appeared on all the coinage. Astley was enormously successful in introducing a form of popular entertainment which appealed to young and old alike, yet his contribution to modern mass entertainment – not just to the circus but to all variety acts both on stage and on television – cries out to be recognised.

There are others who were, in a sense, overshadowed by the achievements of members of the same family. Surely the accolade of greatness would have been bestowed on Marc Isambard Brunel if it were not for the fame subsequently achieved by his son, the engineer Isambard Kingdom Brunel? And would Erasmus Darwin not be famous, a polymath giant of his time, were it not for the subsequent fame of his grandson Charles Darwin?

In a way it is almost as if fame capriciously shines a spotlight on one particular individual and leaves the person standing next to him in total darkness. Look at the fame and reputation of Josiah Wedgwood. Nothing wrong with that – he was a great innovator, marketeer and industrialist. But it is almost as if time has elevated him to the status of being 'the only potter'. Yet there were others just as important – such as Josiah Spode who, after all, gave us the process for manufacturing bone china, and who introduced the blue-on-white transfer printing which so revolutionised the nation's dinner services. No Spode, no willow pattern....

Sometimes fame favours the 'first mover' – the first person to invent something or to achieve a particular thing. In some cases, however, fame falls on the shoulders of the man who implements that change and makes it into a financial success. For this, think of Isaac Singer – the man whose name is synonymous with sewing machines. Did he invent the sewing machine? No, but he infringed the patent of a man called Elias Howe, who in turn had simply 'borrowed' the idea from the original inventor, a Walter Hunt who came up with the idea in 1830s. Hunt had been so horrified that his invention could throw thousands of garment makers out of a job that he declined to take out a patent, but Howe had no such scruples and claimed the idea as his own. And even Hunt had inadvertently borrowed the idea of the lock-stitch from a British inventor called Thomas Saint. He had patented the idea for the sewing machine as far back as 1790, but unfortunately described his invention in such an obscure way that no one understood what it was. Fifty years later, Singer was forced to pay compensation to Howe – but kept the fame. Neither Hunt nor Saint ever got any credit – or even a brass farthing.

Similarly, at school we all learned about Sir Richard Arkwright, a man described in his own lifetime as 'the Father of the Industrial Revolution'. He filed patents for various inventions – only to see them all set aside when it was subsequently determined that he was not in fact the inventor. He claimed credit for inventing the spinning frame – later renaming it the water frame after it was adapted to water power. Yet the ideas for this certainly came from Thomas Highs, with whom he had worked many years previously. Highs never had the financial strength to take out a patent in his own name. And it was Highs who has also been credited with inventing the Spinning Jenny several years before James Hargreaves. That is not to discredit Arkwright entirely, who, after all, introduced modern factory techniques and revolutionised cotton manufacture in the mills of Lancashire. But why should 'the little men' – the Thomas Highs of this world – not get credit for the part they played in contributing to Arkwright's fame and fortune? Highs died a pauper, having been dependent upon the charity of others; Arkwright died with over half a million pounds to his name. Who ever said life was fair?

Some people were popular, but not famous, and yet played their part in inspiring others to achieve greatness. Charles Babbage is rightly acknowledged as the father of computing with the development of his 'Analytical Engine' and 'Differential Machine'. But would his interests have gone in other directions were it not for the fact that as an 8-year-old boy he visited the fabulous premises of Joseph John Merlin, clockmaker extraordinaire? Seeing a dancer pirouette and move in time to music, with all the movements pre-determined by complex machinery, was said to have inspired Babbage in his later researches. Many years later he bought the figure of the dancer from Merlin's estate – a sign of its importance in determining the course of his life's work.

Sometimes it is as if fame reckoned that it could only squeeze one into the limelight – maybe two at a pinch. So, we have those giants of the industrial age, Matthew Boulton and James Watt, still immortalised with their pictures and achievements on our £50 notes. Yet where is the third leg of the trio, William Murdoch, the man who worked with the pair of Boulton and Watt, who invented both the oscillating cylinder steam engine and gas lighting, and refined and developed many of Watt's ideas? Shadowed by fame, obscured by history.

Sometimes the extent of the overshadowing was deliberate, as in the case of William Wilberforce and the abolition movement. Of course Wilberforce was important, but to read his story as written by his family, he was a one-man-band, a dynamo of energy, determination and hard work. But the truth is that Wilberforce was a reluctant campaigner, a man chosen to promote the cause because he was wealthy enough to have bought a seat in the House of Commons. Plagued by self-doubts and frequently propped up by others, he became the figurehead of a revolution – but at the expense of the real hero, the man who worked tirelessly to produce the bullets for Wilberforce to fire; the man who dedicated his whole life to the abolition movement – Thomas Clarkson. To William Wilberforce has gone all the glory; Thomas Clarkson gets barely a footnote in history.

Smeaton and Maudslay are hardly household names – perhaps their specialisms were just too obscure or 'uninteresting'. Yet Smeaton was really the country's first civil engineer, building breakwaters and bridges, harbours and lighthouses – and Maudslay, an engineering perfectionist, gave us standardised nuts and bolts, manufactured to an incredible degree of accuracy, which literally held the Industrial Revolution together.

In the Arts, the spotlight falls on Reynolds, on Gainsborough and to some extent on Constable, although he never sold a single one of his 'big canvasses' in his lifetime. Yet Thomas Lawrence, the doyen of Regency painters, fell into disfavour in the nineteenth century – not because his pictures weren't any good, but because his louche behaviour and personal excesses horrified Victorian sensibilities. He may have been knighted; he may have been able to claim to be 'the man who painted the face of the Regency period' – but he is totally overshadowed nowadays by the artists who came before and after him. Another fine artist, Joseph Wright of Derby, had the nerve to tackle head-on the collision between religion and science, with his paintings of industrial scenes – scenes in which scientific discoveries were shown as being on the same scale as divine revelations.

And what of James Gillray, that acerbic if not vitriolic recorder of the foibles and peccadilloes of others? In a way he was the escape valve for a society which had grown tired of autocratic rule, yet who shied back from following in the footsteps of the French Revolution. A century earlier we had tried regicide. It didn't change a thing. So, thanks to Gillray and others like him, we discovered a better way of bringing our leaders to heel – we ridiculed them. We laughed openly at their misdemeanours, their excesses, their weaknesses, but in doing so, Gillray enabled the world to change itself, to evolve, to adapt.

There are a host of others worthy of inclusion – this is simply a personal choice. But I want it to be more than merely a 'Second Eleven' of eighteenth century successes. I believe that the selection represents people who achieved more than they have been given credit for. They either lived in the shadow of others 250 years ago, or have become dwarfed by their success. Fame blinds, fame hides – it is time for a fairer way of illuminating the past.

Chapter 1

The Ground Breakers

Newcomen's *Engine for Raising Water ... by Fire*, from 1717.

Thomas Newcomen, 1664–1729

In the field of steam power used in eighteenth-century industry, James Watt stands pre-eminent. His is a household name, and it is easy to assume that he was not only the first man to harness steam power effectively, but that his invention came out of nowhere, and then became universally accepted. This was simply not the case, and indeed during the period up to 1800, when the Watt patent expired, only some 450 out of 2,200 steam engines made in Britain followed the designs of James Watt. A far greater number followed the designs of an unsung predecessor, the remarkable Thomas Newcomen. His machines may have been more basic, less powerful and less fuel efficient – but they remained popular because they were cheaper to produce and simpler to maintain.

Newcomen engines dominated the marketplace for three quarters of a century. They were undoubtedly inefficient, unsophisticated and required large quantities of coal. While this may not have been a problem when the machines were being used to pump out water from coal mines, it was a major factor for mine owners in areas such as Cornwall, where metals such as tin and copper were mined and where coal was absent. This meant that coal had to be brought to the site – at considerable expense.

Of course the Watt engine, with its separate condenser, was a technical revolution, but that should not mean that Newcomen is denied credit for paving the way; for bringing into production the first effective steam engine, way back in 1712.

Thomas Newcomen was born in 1664, to a family of merchants in Dartmouth. This Devon town was close to the various mining villages dotted around Dartmoor, and also gave access to the copper and tin mines which dotted the countryside in the adjoining county of Cornwall. This was Newcomen's 'patch', which he would have travelled around as a young man, promoting the ironmongery business which he started in around 1685. Before that, Newcomen had been apprenticed as an engineer in the county town of Exeter.

The young Newcomen would have been well aware of the problems faced by mine owners in trying to prevent mine shafts flooding. Traditionally this meant trying to bale out the flooded mines with buckets, pulleys and ropes. Horse power and manual labour were the only two viable alternatives, although wind power had also been tried, using windmills erected immediately at the head of the mine shaft.

As a young adult Newcomen was selling equipment from his ironmongery shop aimed at helping these mine owners. He did not just sell products made by others – he listened to the mine owners and engineered items specifically for their needs. He was a good engineer, a good listener and a good problem-solver. Like so many of the men featured in this book, Thomas Newcomen was a Dissenter – he was a devout Baptist and a lay preacher. Not only did this mean that he was 'driven', but also that he was unfettered by prevailing views, unwilling to accept that things could not be changed, or that 'this is the way things are: accept it'. Conformity – to Church of England ideas and to mainstream thinking – seemed to suffocate others, whereas Nonconformists were willing to challenge, to embrace new ideas and, in that ghastly modern phrase, to think outside the box. This entrepreneurial spirit dominated so many of the earlier inventors and advocators of change and Newcomen was no exception.

He was not by any means the first to advocate steam power. Early attempts had been made by men such as Edward Somerset, Thomas Savery and Denis Papin. They had all worked on various schemes to use fire to heat water in order to create a vacuum. Most of these early ideas remained simply that – ideas. What Newcomen did was to put them into practice – to make a machine which could be taken to the head of the mine, erected, fired up, and then used to pump water.

Probably because Cornwall had no coal to fire up the engine, the early experiments took place not where Newcomen lived, but close to the collieries of the Midlands and as far north as Yorkshire. The first may well have been at Griff colliery in Warwickshire (1711); followed up by installations at Bilston in Staffordshire (1714); at Hawarden in Flintshire (1715); at Austhorpe in West Yorkshire (1715) and at Whitehaven in Cumberland (1715).

At this stage Newcomen was in partnership with another Dartmoor resident, a man called John Calley (variously described as a glassmaker and a plumber). Much of their experimentation was 'hit and miss' – they were not developing a well-researched theoretical concept based on detailed figures and calculations, and it was a case of trying different ideas until they found one which worked. In practice, Calley disappeared from the scene before he could see the success of their venture – he died in 1715.

The following year Newcomen was granted a patent for his steam-driven pumping engine. *The London Gazette* reported:

Whereas the invention for raising water by the impellant force of fire, authorized by Parliament, is lately brought to the greatest perfection, and all sorts of mines, etc., may be thereby drained and water raised to any height with more ease and less charge than by the other methods hitherto used, as is sufficiently demonstrated by diverse engines of this invention now at work in the several counties of Stafford, Warwick, Cornwall, and Flint. These are therefore, to give notice that if any person shall be desirous to treat with the proprietors for such engines, attendance will be given for that purpose every Wednesday at the Sword Blade Coffee House in Birchin Lane, London.

In practice the partnership of Newcomen/Calley must have been working on the experiments for some years. A Swedish visitor to England by the name of Marten Triewald wrote in 1717 to describe his acquaintanceship with the pair of inventors – he had apparently observed them assembling their 'fire machine' at Byker Colliery near Newcastle upon Tyne. In his words:

> *Now it happened that a man from Dartmouth named* Thomas Newcomen, ... *made up his mind in conjunction with his assistant, a plumber by the name of* Calley, *to invent a fire machine for drawing water from the mines. He was induced to undertake this by considering the heavy cost of lifting water by means of horses, which he found existing in the English tin mines. These mines* Mr Newcomen *often visited in the capacity of a dealer in iron tools with which he used to furnish many of the tin mines ... For ten consecutive years* Mr Newcomen *worked at this fire-machine.*

What comes across was what a thoroughly decent man Newcomen was; mine owners wrote of his scrupulous business arrangements and his unfailing honesty. Many of these owners may have been fellow-Baptists – they trusted Newcomen and they swiftly spread word of his 'fire machines' among other owners. In a comparatively short time, over 100 engines had been put to use. At that stage they had limited effectiveness in that they could only operate in comparatively shallow mine workings, at a time when mine owners were driving ever-deeper shafts.

Perhaps it was his innate decency that meant that Newcomen was willing to pay Savery's estate a share of the profits, choosing not to argue that there were significant differences between his own invention and the one described in Savery's patent nearly twenty years earlier. Savery had demonstrated his ideas to the Royal Society in 1699 having taken out a fourteen-year patent the year before, covering his invention for 'raising water and imparting motion to all sorts of mill-work by the impellant force of fire, useful for draining mines, serving towns with water and working all kinds of mills in cases where there is neither water nor constant wind.' This patent was then extended by twenty-one years, expiring in 1733. Newcomen accepted that Savery had appeared first on the scene. Presumably he would have known Savery, who lived at Totnes just a few miles from Newcomen's hometown. No matter that Savery had never successfully produced a working example, or that one of his attempts caught fire and exploded. No matter that it was Newcomen who added the 'missing ingredient' – a way of condensing the steam in the cylinder by injecting cold water from an external tank. No matter that in order to work, the Savery design would have had to go beyond the limits of seventeenth-century technology. Also, Savery's machine could only have pumped water from a depth of 30ft, whereas Newcomen's development meant that the machine could be used to pump out 10 gallons of water every minute, from a depth of up to 156ft.

Despite these obvious differences, the upshot was that instead of litigation and rancour, an unincorporated company called 'The Proprietors of the Invention for Raising Water by Fire' was formed to share the profits, and it pressed ahead with a series of installations and improvements. Even after the ideas of James Watt and John Smeaton had led to radical improvements to steam engines, the basic Newcomen engine remained in use, for many years, the 'workhorse' of the first part of the Industrial Revolution. Many were adapted to incorporate Watt's idea for a condenser – giving rise to a hybrid described as a 'pickle-pot' condenser. In all, it is thought that some 2,000 Newcomen engines were sold in England and on the Continent during the eighteenth and nineteenth centuries.

Newcomen had married in 1705, when he was 41. His bride was another Devonian, one Hannah Waymouth. She bore him three children, all of whom reached adulthood. Although little is known about his later years, Newcomen remained active in promoting his engines, before finally dying, in London, on 5 August 1729. He was buried in the Dissenters Burial Ground at Bunhill Fields – the same cemetery where the mortal remains of other prominent Nonconformists, such as Daniel Defoe, William Blake and John Bunyan, are interred.

There is no gravestone marking Newcomen's burial, no impressive mausoleum telling the world that a great man lies buried beneath. In a way, that sums up Thomas Newcomen: a thoroughly worthy, honest guy who was pleased to help mine owners cope with a problem which was affecting their business; who counted his clients as his friends, and who recognised that he was just one part of a jigsaw. He was no Arkwright, claiming credit for the inventions of others. He never achieved great fame in his lifetime, and nothing suggests that he lived an opulent lifestyle or died rich. His children achieved solid middle-class respectability: one developing a business making serge cloth (used in making military costumes, trench coats and so on); another running an ironmongery shop; and another marrying a surgeon. Newcomen played a crucial part in 'getting the ball rolling'. His atmospheric engine was not perfect, but that alone inspired others to make improvements and to give impetus to the Industrial Revolution.

A modified version of the Newcomen engine is still on display in Dartmouth, albeit using hydraulic rather than steam power, and there is another in the Science Museum. Various others can be found elsewhere in museums both in Britain and overseas. The Newcomen Society does its best to maintain and promote Newcomen's reputation and in 2012 the Royal Mail brought out a stamp featuring Newcomen's steam engine as part its 'Britons of Distinction' series.

Richard Trevithick, 1771–1833

It was Christmas Eve, 1801 and a large crowd had gathered in the Cornish town of Camborne. The stretch of road running up from Tehidy Road and along Fore Street was known as Camborne Hill, and the crowds watched in amazement as a noisy, steam-belching leviathan called 'Puffing Devil' moved slowly up the ascent, turned round, and then came back down again. The excitement of the occasion was described by a local cooper, Stephen Williams, who was to write later:

> 'Twas a stiffish hill going from the Weith up to Camborne Beacon, but she went off like a little bird. When she had gone about a quarter of a mile, there was a roughish piece of road covered with loose stones; she didn't go quite so fast, and as it was flood of rain and we were very squeezed together, I jumped off. She was going faster than I could walk, and went on up the hill about a quarter or half a mile farther, when they turned her and came back again to the shop.

The event was commemorated in the song *Camborne Hill*:

> Goin' up Camborne Hill, coming down
> Goin' up Camborne Hill, coming down
> The horses stood still;
> The wheels went around;
> Going up Camborne Hill coming down

It is a song still associated with Cornish prowess – especially on the rugby field – and is one of the most lasting tributes to a man who died a pauper, and yet was a real pioneer of the Industrial Revolution. His name – Richard Trevithick – is little known nowadays, and as any schoolboy will tell you, the inventor of steam locomotion was not Trevithick but father and son George and Robert Stephenson. Actually, that is not correct. The Stephenson 'Rocket' may be renowned the world over, whereas Trevithick's 'Catch-me-who-can' engine is hardly remembered. Yet it was the first in the world to carry fee-paying passengers, in 1808. The 'Rocket' is rightly famous for having won the Rainhill Trials held to decide the best design for an engine to run along the Liverpool–Manchester line. Yet that was in 1829, a quarter of a century after Trevithick had pioneered the use of a high-pressure steam engine to provide locomotive power. Trevithick's invention came first, and he deserves far more credit for his inventiveness and his dogged determination. Indeed, he can be seen as one of the first of a breed of heroic failures littering the story of modern progress.

Trevithick was a gentle giant of a man – well over 6ft tall, born in the parish of Illogan in Cornwall in April 1771 and educated – somewhat sparsely – at a local elementary school. At school, when he bothered to turn up, he developed a reputation for cussedness and disobedience. Nowadays he would probably be diagnosed as having Attention Deficit Syndrome, not least because he was actually quite bright, quick witted and good with figures. As the youngest of six children born to a Cornish mining family, his horizons must have appeared to be limited to the local mining community – and yet he turned out to be able to fly much farther afield. He was generally popular as a youngster and earned the nickname of the Cornish Giant because of his size and strength. What also singled him out was that he was an extremely practical man – good at problem solving. It was a time of great opportunity in the Cornish mining community, not least because after 1800 the patents taken out by James Watt had expired, meaning that mine owners were free to make their own experiments to adapt and improve on the existing machinery. In this environment Trevithick was able to spend time tweaking and altering the existing machines, improving their fuel efficiency and thereby reducing running costs. He was soon in high demand throughout Cornwall, where he was looked on as something of a local hero – a man who was soon in direct competition with the 'outsider' James Watt, who was keen to avoid losing his dominance in the manufacture of pumping machines.

Watt had always championed low-pressure engines – they were cheaper to produce, less temperamental and indeed less likely to explode. They were also virtually silent because they relied on condensing steam to produce a vacuum. Trevithick was determined to develop a high-pressure machine, with the advantage that it used far less coal and hence was particularly appropriate to be used in Cornwall as it reduced the need for transporting coal from far afield. It introduced to the world the noise of steam escaping rhythmically – giving rise to the name of 'puffer' for his machines. These machines were initially used as static engines operating winding gear. There were occasional problems, such as in 1803 when one of Trevithick's high-pressure engines exploded. Such instances were immediately seized upon by Watt, and by his partner Matthew Bolton, as evidence of how pressurised steam was inherently dangerous. Undeterred, Trevithick set about introducing safety features and modifications. His experiments culminated in the production of what became known as the 'Cornish boiler' – using a horizontal cylinder with a single fire-tube running through the centre. It is sometimes referred to as an internally fired boiler, and in its basic form, it remained in use well into the twentieth century. Trevithick was not the only pioneer to try and harness power using high-pressure steam – but he was the first to do so successfully in an industrial context. His were no theoretical examples – they actually worked.

Meanwhile, Trevithick also worked on the idea for an engine which could drive wheels, generating locomotive power – hence the Camborne Hill experiment in 1801. It was not wholly without incident – the drivers apparently were so pleased with their efforts that a couple of days later, having driven down Camborne Hill, they retired to the local hostelry to celebrate, leaving the steam engine unattended and without topping up the water levels. While they quaffed their ale and ate their Christmas goose the engine overheated, caught fire and was seriously damaged. Undeterred, Trevithick applied for, and obtained, a patent for his steam locomotive in March 1802. The next year saw a Trevithick locomotive, known as the London Steam Carriage, being demonstrated in London to astonished onlookers. It ran between Holborn and Paddington. It was however far too heavy for the ground over which it travelled and had the added disadvantage of being uncomfortable for passengers and, even worse, was more expensive than travelling by horse.

More tragically, in 1803 another of Trevithick's machines was being demonstrated in Greenwich when an explosion occurred, killing four people. Trevithick responded by developing safety valves to prevent the build-up of excessive pressure, as well as a manometer so that the operator could read the pressure inside the boiler.

Trevithick then took a job as engineer at Penydarren ironworks, near Merthyr Tydfil. In early 1804 he started to experiment with an engine towing wagons, culminating in a trial on 21 February when his engine hauled a 10-ton load of iron for a distance of 9½ miles over a period of slightly more than four hours. The average speed – at around 2½ miles an hour – may not seem impressive, but it established for the first time that steam locomotion was feasible and could be used to move significant amounts of freight. Trevithick was to write of the events of that day:

> … *yesterday we proceeded on our journey with the engine, and we carried ten tons of iron in five wagons, and seventy men riding on them the whole of the journey… the engine, while working, went nearly five miles an hour; there was no water put into the boiler from the time we started until our journey's end… the coal consumed was two hundredweight.*

The demonstration was an undoubted success, even though a bolt on the boiler sheared off on the return journey, which was made with empty wagons, and this meant that the fire had to be allowed to go out and the journey was postponed until the following day.

One of Trevithick's sponsors, a Mr Samuel Homfray, allegedly won 500 guineas as a result of the successful experiment – a reminder that the Georgians would gamble on anything which moved. Impressed, Mr Homfray bought out a one tenth share in Trevithick's patent for steam locomotion. However, there was little further progress made on the Penydarren site because the ground was too soft to carry the heavy load imposed on it. Perhaps this was not surprising, since the track had been designed for use by much lighter, horse-drawn, loads. The wagons derailed and the engine was relegated to static use, to drive a forge hammer used in the ironmaking process.

That was not entirely the end of Trevithick's experiments with locomotion. In July and August 1808 Londoners could see his engine 'Catch-me-who-can' travel around a circuit on rails. For a payment of 1 shilling they could board the train for a ride, which operated near Gower Street, close to the modern-day Euston Square Underground Station. A wooden palisade had been erected around the site to deter 'rubber neckers' and to maximise profits, but the venture was not a financial success. Once again, the ground – and the track being used on it – was not up to the job and a derailment followed a split in the rail and caused the project to be abandoned. Thereafter, Trevithick appears to have lost interest in his 'toy', although his assistant John Steele took the technology up to the North-east of England, building a locomotive at the Wylam Colliery 10 miles to the west of Newcastle in 1805. Once more, the track proved inadequate for the weight of the locomotive, but it was significant in that the experimental track for the first time used flanged rails to assist adhesion. Thereafter developments lay in the hands of the Stephensons – George Stephenson had been born in Wylam, and by 1814 he had produced his own locomotive, the Blücher.

The installation of static engines had continued throughout this period, especially in Cornwall where it is estimated that by 1804 between twelve and fourteen engines had been installed to operate the winding gear. But Trevithick's attention was beginning to wander into other fields and in 1805 he showed that a canal barge could be driven by a paddle wheel powered by steam. The following year he introduced three steam-powered dredgers onto the River Thames. He was constantly examining opportunities for extending the purposes to which steam power could be put –crushing stones, operating forge hammers, boring-out brass cylinders for cannon manufacture and as blast-furnace blowers. In 1807 he formed a partnership with Robert Dickinson to produce a floating crane, called the Nautical Labourer, propelled by steam-driven paddle wheels. Opposition from dock workers worried about their jobs ensured that the venture never succeeded – and Trevithick himself received death threats for his efforts.

It marked a period of failed enterprises. In 1807 he had joined the Thames Archway Company to build the Thames Drift Tunnel; he had been called in as engineer after the project had got no further than the digging of the two end shafts, either side of the Thames at Rotherhithe. With Trevithick's help, the horizontal shaft was started, using a pilot tunnel. But after around 300 yards disaster struck: on two occasions the tunnel flooded when the roof fell in. The second time it happened, Trevithick was lucky to escape with his life. The project was abandoned and a tunnel under the Thames only became a reality in 1843, after Isambard Marc Brunel (mentioned later in this chapter) had come up with his revolutionary tunnel-boring machine. Brunel constructed his Rotherhithe Tunnel just three quarters of a mile from the spot where Trevithick had failed.

Trevithick then moved on and tinkered with ways of raising wrecks from the seabed by pumping air into iron tanks strapped to the wreck; he experimented with ways of using a ship's boilers to provide heat for cooking; he proposed iron ship-buoys and came up with ideas for telescopic iron masts, iron floating-docks and so on. None of the ideas were money-spinners and in February 1811, both Trevithick and his partner Robert Dickinson were declared bankrupt. Clearing those debts took Trevithick three years but it did not prevent him from returning to Cornwall to make further developments to the 'Cornish engines', notably at the Wheal Prosper Mine. His machines were also adapted for agricultural use, with his steam threshing machine appearing in 1812 in fields at Probus in Cornwall. For over seventy years the machine operated successfully – and with considerable cost savings over using horse- and manpower. His powered plough was less of a triumph and his 1812 invention of a screw propeller for marine propulsion never materialised. He applied for a patent, gave instructions for the first propeller to be cast – but then lost interest and went off to Peru to seek his fortune working in the silver mines.

It was a strange decision, but it followed a visit to England by Peruvian mine owner Francisco Uville in 1811. His mines were at high altitude, meaning that the Boulton and Watt low-pressure condensing engines were unable to operate. Uville had bought a Trevithick high-pressure engine, shipped it to Peru, and found that it worked well. He persuaded Trevithick to make the journey and in 1816 Trevithick left Penzance on board the whaling ship *Asp* – and didn't return for eleven years. Poor Mrs Trevithick; she had married Richard in 1797 and was left behind with her six children, the youngest of whom was less than a year old when father disappeared over the horizon. Not one silver penny was paid her by her husband during his entire Peruvian adventure and she had to survive on the generosity of her brother.

The Peruvian venture developed into an unmitigated disaster – Trevithick quickly fell out with Uville and although he secured an appointment as a mining consultant and travelled extensively around the country, he did not have the capital to invest in new mines himself, apart from a copper and silver mine at Caxatambo. But these were troubled times, and the nascent independence movement, led by Simon Bolivar, resulted in continual problems with the resident Spanish army.

Finally, he had to abandon his mine at Caxatambo, along with the ore which he had already extracted and which was worth some £5,000 – roughly £3 million in modern monetary terms. He headed for Costa Rica and dabbled in the idea of constructing a railway across the Isthmus of Panama, but was lucky to escape with his life on several occasions. Travel was extremely hazardous and after a close encounter with a crocodile and a near-drowning, Trevithick finally reached Cartegena in Columbia, penniless and starving, in 1827. There he had a fortuitous meeting with Robert Stephenson, son of George. Robert was on his way home from Columbia and apparently had little in common with Trevithick, who had last met him when Robert was a baby. Nevertheless, Robert lent Trevithick £50 to cover his return to England, and Trevithick landed at Falmouth on 9 October 1827.

His mind appears to have been fully occupied during the return journey and before long he was proposing a recoil gun carriage. In 1828 he visited Holland to look at ways of draining the polders, and in 1830 came up with an idea for a room storage heater. This worked on the basis of heating water in a container, which could then be wheeled from room to room. The release of heat could then be controlled by the use of adjustable doors. His final patent was taken out in March 1833, when he produced ideas for further improvements to steam engines, in their application to navigation and locomotion.

At this stage Trevithick was living in the Dartford area of London, but in the spring of 1833 he caught pneumonia and died on the morning of 22 April. He was destitute and his work colleagues had to raise funds to facilitate his burial. He ended up interred in an unmarked grave at St Edmund's Burial Ground, East Hill, Dartford. The site was closed in the 1850s and a small plaque records the fact that Trevithick lies buried nearby. He had just celebrated his sixty-second birthday when he died.

A reminder of the mind-blowing nature of his inventions can be seen from this excerpt from the *Gloucester Journal* of 27 February 1804. Describing the events at the Penydarren Ironworks the paper enthused:

The expence of fire to generate the ordinary pressure of steam does not exceed one cwt. of coal (to each horse power required) in the 24 hours: its action creates a pleasing astonishment, not being fettered with either condenser or air pump, and one simple cock or valve governing its whole motion; neither is it encumbered with the heavy gearing attached to most other engines…. To those who are not acquainted with the exact principle of this new engine, it may not be improper to observe, that it differs from all others yet brought before the public, by disclaiming the use of condensing water, and discharges its steam into the open air, or applies it to the use of heating of fluids, as conveniency may require. …It is only necessary to supply a small quantity of water for the purpose of creating the steam, which is a most essential matter. It performed the journey without feeding the boiler or using any water, and will travel with ease at the rate of five miles an hour.

Succeeding generations may have overlooked Trevithick's remarkable contribution to rail travel, but his contemporaries were under no doubt. He helped bring about a revolution in travel, and his brilliance has never been adequately recognised. Not that lack of recognition really troubled the man – he wrote to his fellow-engineer Davies Gilbert, saying:

I have been branded with folly and madness for attempting what the world calls impossibilities, and even from the great engineer, the late Mr. James Watt, who said to an eminent scientific character still living, that I deserved hanging for bringing into use the high-pressure engine. This so far has been my reward from the public; but should this be all, I shall be satisfied by the great secret pleasure and laudable pride that I feel in my own breast from having been the instrument of bringing forward and maturing new principles and new arrangements of boundless value to my country. However much I may be straitened in pecuniary circumstances, the great honour of being a useful subject can never be taken from me, which to me far exceeds riches.

A noble sentiment – and a fine epitaph to an extraordinarily talented man.

John Smeaton, 1724–1798

The name 'Smeaton' may be revered among engineers, but is hardly a household name. At best, people may know that John Smeaton was 'something to do with lighthouses', and yet he really was a remarkable engineer with incredibly diverse interests and achievements. He cut his teeth on windmills and waterwheels, working out scientifically their power and effectiveness. He analysed steam engines, making improvements to the early Newcomen engines and working out ways to measure their performance accurately. He designed bridges and canals; he advised on schemes for harbours and coastal protection walls. He studied the 'physics' of cement, not only coming up with a mixture which was quick-drying and could be used under water, but also setting out the principles which would eventually lead to modern 'Portland' cement. He worked out a way to dovetail solid granite blocks, pegged with marble, to create a structure which could withstand a hundred years of being battered by the sea. He devised a scheme to raise those blocks 18 metres in the air, from a moving (floating) base so that those stones could be put in place atop the Eddystone Lighthouse.

In carrying out this wide range of work he declared that it was different to that carried out by military engineers, and named his area of expertise 'civil engineering' to mark that difference. In many senses, therefore, he can be described as the father of civil engineering. He was both the product of the Industrial Revolution, and one of its architects.

Smeaton was born on 8 June 1724 at Austhorpe in Leeds. He attended the local grammar school and was then articled in his father's law firm. But the law held few attractions for the lad, and he left the firm in order to become a maker of scientific instruments, working with the great watch and clockmaker Henry Hindley. At the age of 24 he set up business in Great Turnstile in the Holborn area of London, making scientific instruments, and he soon developed a vacuum pump which was superior to anything seen previously. He also collaborated in working on a new form of compass, and in 1750 this underwent sea-trials with the Royal Navy before being accepted as the standard issue on all naval ships. In time he also designed and made telescopes, and a precision lathe.

His success meant that he was employing three men and he soon needed larger premises, moving to Furnival Inn Court at the end of 1751. Throughout his time in London he kept a keen interest in the progress of building Westminster Bridge – only the second crossing over the Thames. Building the bridge had started in 1739, funded in part by lottery money, and in many ways it was a poorly designed structure with inherent weaknesses. These had become apparent in 1746 when one of the bridge piers started to subside. Two years later, Smeaton submitted a proposal for a coffer dam to be erected so that repairs could be carried out and this seemed to kickstart his general interest in what he called 'enginery'. By 1753 he was convinced that this was the direction his career should take – as a consultant to building projects, especially involving bridges. During his lifetime a dozen of his bridges were completed, all but two of them in stone. Most still survive to this day. Initially he met with little success – his designs for Blackfriars Bridge and Glasgow Bridge were rejected, but this did not deter him: he published a paper on bridge design. This emphasised the importance of firm foundations for the bridge piers so as to counteract the risk of the riverbed being scoured away and exposing the footings. In particular, he advocated the use of rubble to be applied to the riverbed around each supporting pier, so as to reduce the scouring effects. This was tried successfully with his plans for the five-arch Coldstream Bridge over the River Tweed, designed by Smeaton in 1763 and completed in 1767. Similar designs, but with a different number of arches, were then rolled out for other bridges, the Perth and Tay Bridges for instance. In the case of his design for the first Newark Bridge, built in 1770 over the flood plain of the River Trent, seventy-four arches were required.

Quite separately from designing bridges the length and breadth of the country, Smeaton had developed an interest in windmills and water wheels, especially in terms of evaluating their efficiency. Rigorous experiments, sometimes using scale models, were carried out to see exactly how much power was being generated with different designs. In 1759 he presented his findings to the Royal Society, of which he was a Fellow, and was awarded the prestigious Copley Medal in recognition of the importance of his work. He subsequently put this knowledge into practice, designing some sixty new mills – mostly watermills but also including half-a-dozen windmills and a couple of horse-drawn mills.

Smeaton also wanted to test the efficiency of Newcomen's steam engines (see earlier) and came up with a number of design modifications which significantly improved their performance and efficiency. He approached the problem with a suitably scientific analysis: he personally carried out site visits to more than a dozen of the most efficient Newcomen engines and carried out detailed measurements. He constructed his own engine to use as a test model and in time was able to come up with an engine which was 25 per cent more efficient than any previous one. Indeed, he was the first person to write in terms of horsepower – the measure of work carried out by a horse in the course of an eight-hour day. This was in 1765, and the idea became central to Watt's own definition of horsepower, which he propounded some eighteen years later. Smeaton designed and sold more than a dozen pumping machines. Later, when the condenser designed by James Watt marked a radical departure for steam engine design, and made Smeaton's tweaks and modifications obsolete, Smeaton was among the first to congratulate Watt, and was the man who proposed his admission as a Fellow of the Royal Society in 1785.

Back in 1753 Smeaton developed an interest in land drainage schemes, and visited the Low Countries where the Dutch had had several centuries of experience in using windmills, dykes, sluices and artificial watercourses to convert swampy low-lying land into useful farmland. Fired up by this visit, and using his own knowledge of measuring water flow, he came up with ideas for three major fen-drainage schemes and a number of canal proposals. The largest of these was the Forth and Clyde Canal, which was started in 1768 and completed in 1777, crossing the whole of Scotland from east to west.

However, the scheme which really showed his engineering skills at their best was his involvement with the Eddystone Lighthouse. The dangerous rocky outcrop, some ten miles off the Devon coast, had long been a danger to shipping in the English Channel. Two earlier wooden lighthouses had been erected. The first, Winstanley's lighthouse, was destroyed in the Great Storm of 1703. The second, designed by John Rudyerd, was built in 1709 but caught fire and was destroyed in December 1755. Replacing this was an absolute priority and it is a measure of the reputation of Smeaton, then aged 31, that he was recommended by the President of the Royal Society to come up with designs for a new lighthouse, early in 1756.

Smeaton's design involved a granite tower erected using an intricate jigsaw of interlocking blocks, held in place by marble 'dowel rods' known as joggles. Rather than 'plane' the rocky base smooth, Smeaton preferred to have the lowest row of blocks carved to make an exact fit. Each course had to be assembled first on dry land, and shipping the materials out to the site could only take place in the summer months. All site work had to be suspended in the winter because access onto the rocks was impossible. The skills used in carving the blocks were of the highest order, and Smeaton personally checked the quarries where the granite was extracted to ensure that only the best materials were used.

He also had to design an ingenious method of raising the blocks from the moving platform of a ship, up onto the growing tower. It still left the problem of coming up with a cement to fix the blocks and act as a grout. Undeterred, Smeaton experimented with a quick drying cement, essential in the wet conditions on the rock, and the same formula is still used today. He was helped in his researches by the chemist William Cookworthy, pioneer of English porcelain. By mixing lime with equal portions of volcanic ash, and using either seawater or fresh water (it made no difference) Smeaton was able to finish his tower, some 37 metres above sea level, in September 1759. It was topped by a lantern cupola containing two counter-balanced chandeliers, each with a dozen candles. These were first lit in October of that year – and the lighthouse remained in use until 1877 when cracks appeared in the underlying rocks, caused by hidden caves beneath the surface. The upper part of Smeaton's tower was dismantled and re-erected over a two-year period on Plymouth Hoe. The 'stump', being solid and made to such a high standard, proved too difficult to move and remains to this day alongside the replacement lighthouse put up by Trinity House and opened in 1882.

From working offshore, Smeaton moved on to designing breakwaters, dry docks and general harbour improvements. There were more than thirty such proposals and although many of these never got further than the drawing board, the fact remained that Smeaton, supported by a small number of colleagues and disciples, was changing the face of Britain. There were setbacks – in particular after Smeaton's design for Hexham Bridge proved to be defective. The piers for the bridge were constructed on inadequate foundations – ironic, considering Smeaton's expertise in such matters, and when the river was in flood in 1782 it washed away six of the supporting piers. It was a humiliating failure for Smeaton, who felt compelled to write to the resident engineer Jonathan Pickernell in the aftermath of the failure, sadly saying: 'All our honours are now in the dust! It cannot now be said, that in the course of 30 years' practice ... not one of Smeaton's works has failed.' This hammer blow to his pride – and reputation – was followed by a dropping-off in commissions.

Worse was to follow: a year after the Hexham Bridge disaster, Smeaton's wife fell seriously ill and died in January 1784 at the age of 59. Smeaton was devastated, and retired from all forms of civil engineering for a period of three years. However, when he returned as a consultant engineer it was with a flourish – bridges, harbours, breakwaters and canals all followed.

Smeaton had a wonderful way of inspiring others around him, always willing to see how things worked, whether they could be improved and so on. He had inherited Austhorpe Lodge near Leeds, built by his grandfather, and mothballed by his father. He set about constructing a tall tower for use as his consultancy studio – with a forge downstairs in the basement, a lathe on the floor above, a floor for his models and then a floor used for his drawing room and study, topped off by an attic area used for storage – and Smeaton's astronomical studies. Once he was immersed in his studies he was never to be disturbed. It was his practice to start each project with a sketch, which he would hand over to his two draughtsmen to have developed into detailed drawings.

Smeaton pioneered fixed fees for routine commissions – 25 guineas for a water mill, 30 guineas for a windmill. Customers were charged 1 guinea for a consultation at Austhorpe, double that 'if sent for', and 5 guineas if he was required to spend the day in London. In 1771 he became one of the founder members of the Society of Civil Engineers – a fortnightly dining club for engineers and scientists to meet and discuss current ideas. Upon his death it was renamed the Smeatonian Society – a name it has kept to this day.

On 16 September 1792 Smeaton suffered a stroke while walking in his garden at Austhorpe. He recovered his mental faculties and was aware of his physical incapacity, ruefully remarking: 'It could not be otherwise; the shadows must lengthen as the sun goes down'. He died on 28 October and is buried in the parish church of St Mary's, Whitkirk, in West Yorkshire. *The Gentleman's Magazine* contained his obituary: 'As a civil engineer, Mr. Smeaton was not equalled by any of the age he lived in: it may, perhaps be added, by none of any previous age.' More than 225 years later, the encomium can happily be extended – Smeaton remains unequalled in the history of civil engineering. He was the first, and possibly the most influential, of his entire profession.

Marc Isambard Brunel, 1769–1849

There has only ever been room for one Brunel in the panoply of great engineers – and that is Isambard Kingdom Brunel. And that happens to be rather hard on his father, Marc Isambard Brunel.

Brunel senior was born on 25 April 1769 in the small hamlet of Hacqueville in northern France, the son of a prosperous farmer by the name of Jean Charles Brunel. His mother was Marie Victoria and she was the second of Jean Charles's four wives. An elder brother was expected to inherit the family estates, and Marc Isambard was marked out for a career in the priesthood. He showed no interest in becoming a clergyman however, and went to stay with relatives in Rouen to learn the rudiments of ships and sailing. As a young boy he showed an early aptitude for mechanics, as well as for mathematics and drawing. He was also good at carpentry. In 1786 he joined the navy as a cadet, making several visits to the West Indies. In 1793, with revolutionary fervour threatening to get completely out of hand, he had travelled to Paris to see for himself the upheavals that were marking the trial of Louis XVI. He was imprudent enough to make insensitive remarks about the revolutionary leader Robespierre and was forced to leave Paris in a hurry. Returning to Rouen he met a young English girl called Sophia Kingdom, who was working as a governess. She was the youngest of sixteen children, fathered by William Kingdom, a contracting agent for the army and navy. The family had originally lived in Plymouth, but her father died when she was 8, and she was sent to France to improve her language skills. When she met Brunel the couple fell in love, but he was forced to leave her behind when he had to flee from France, aware that his royalist sympathies were putting his life in grave danger.

He escaped to the new United States of America on board the *Liberty*, arriving on 6 September 1793. In time he developed a busy practice as an architect and civil engineer, designing buildings, constructing a cannon foundry and arsenal, and advising on various canal projects. One of his unsuccessful commissions was for the design of the US Capitol Building in Washington, DC. When he was 27 he was appointed New York city's chief engineer, but when he hit on an idea for manufacturing ship's pulleys via mechanical means (as opposed to being made by hand) he decided to come to England to see if he could interest the Admiralty in backing his project. This was for nothing less than the mass-production of the wooden blocks used in their tens of thousands by the Royal Navy. Brunel got the contract in 1803, installed his machines at Portsmouth and sat back and watched as the factory's forty-three machines, operated by a workforce of just ten men, churned out pulley blocks by the thousand, a process which would previously have needed a hundred men. Brunel used machines designed and made by Henry Maudslay, mentioned in the next chapter. It was a milestone in mechanised mass production, and one which reportedly saved the navy £24,000 a year in production costs. Unfortunately for Brunel, the navy was somewhat dilatory in paying; Brunel had laid out over £2,000 of his own money in order to set up the project. In 1808 the Admiralty agreed to pay £1,000 on account, and followed this up with another instalment of some £17,000 two years later. To put the figures in context: the Admiralty used over 100,000 of these pulley blocks every year, and this new method of production was a highly significant advance.

Brunel had arrived in Britain on 7 March 1799 and immediately sent for Sophia Kingdom, the orphan girl he had first met in Rouen some years earlier. She had endured a terrifying few years, imprisoned under suspicion of being a foreign spy and she probably only escaped with her life because Robespierre had died in July 1794. The couple married on 1 November 1799. Daughters Sophia and Emma swiftly followed, followed by a son, Isambard Kingdom, on 9 April 1806.

Brunel extended his business interests, acquiring a sawmill at Wandsworth, developing a pantograph for copying drawings (which he forgot to patent) and in designing woodworking machines. The sawmill premises were badly damaged by fire in 1814, causing a considerable loss. He was a prolific inventor and his next venture was when he came up with the idea of making machine-stitched boots for use throughout the British Army. When peace with France was declared in 1815 he was left high and dry, with unsold stock. Suddenly no one was buying army boots and this added to his financial woes. A spell in Debtors Prison followed the collapse of his various ventures in 1821, but after three months his friends raised the necessary funds from the government to clear his debts and secure his release. Up until that time he was considering travelling to Russia to work for the Tsar, but the payment of £5,000 was conditional upon Brunel abandoning that plan and staying in England.

There followed a number of business ventures: he looked at ships which could navigate the Thames and proposed a steam tug; he came up with ideas for machines to be used for printing textiles; he used his civil engineering skills to produce bridges, floating landing stages and dry docks. Then came the engineering masterpiece which defined his career – the design for a tunnelling shield to be used in constructing the world's first successful tunnel under a navigable river – in this case, the Thames. In the early 1820s a proposal had been hatched for a tunnel between Wapping and Rotherhithe, and the scheme received parliamentary approval in 1823. Brunel was made chief engineer.

The work necessitated the development of a revolutionary building shield, one which was self-propelled using hydraulic jacks. Brunel came up with the design, and got Maudslay to build it. The rectangular shield consisted of twelve cells, arranged as four rows wide and three rows high. Each cell was intended to be the working area for one man digging at the tunnel face and as fast as the men dug out the tunnel, the bricklayers came behind and lined the newly exposed area with bricks.

It was a revolutionary design and there were a number of teething problems, matched by funding difficulties since the government had made it clear that no taxpayers' money would be provided. Brunel had expected to be tunnelling through London clay: instead he hit sand and gravel. Both had the disadvantage of allowing water to permeate through to the tunnel and on 12 January 1828, a major collapse occurred, causing the tunnel to flood. Six men drowned in the roof collapse and Brunel was lucky not to have been one of them. At that stage some 549ft of tunnel had been dug – not even halfway. Work was held up, not for months, but for seven years. Eventually the government agreed to come up with a loan of nearly a quarter of a million pounds to enable construction to be restarted.

The original tunnelling shield had been damaged and had to be replaced, this time with a machine nearly twice as heavy and involving thousands of parts, all of which had to be assembled underground. Some of the improvements to the shield were proposed by Marc's son Isambard – the two often compared notes and shared problems. Indeed, during the lay-off period Marc had assisted his son in his design work for the Clifton Suspension Bridge. In a similar vein, when the stress of the tunnelling works got too much for Marc, forcing him to take time off from the project, much of the day-to-day work at the tunnel was supervised by the younger Brunel.

The tunnel had started from the southern, i.e. Rotherhithe, side of the Thames. The horizontal shaft progressed beneath the river and in 1840 work started on the Wapping shaft. The two sections slowly approached each other, and met up in December in the following year. Finishing the tunnel involved a mountain of bricks, with each foot of tunnel requiring 5,500 bricks, That made for a total of over 7½ million bricks in all, lining a tunnel 1,300ft long and 35ft wide. Two years were spent installing lighting, the carriageway and spiral staircases. The intention had been to open the tunnel to vehicular traffic, but funds ran out and there was no money to pay for access ramps for the horse-drawn vehicles to use. So, it opened as a tunnel solely for pedestrians, on 25 March 1843. It proved to be a popular venue, with more than a million people crossing under the Thames in the first four months. Shops and kiosks lined the structure and for a while it became a somewhat unlikely must-see attraction for visitors to the capital, the London Eye of its day with over 2 million people a year paying their one penny entrance fee. It was, however, a financial disaster, with the ticket receipts coming nowhere near the construction costs of £634,000. In time, the tunnel became the haunt of pickpockets and prostitutes, and it seemed that Brunel's masterpiece would end up as a complete white elephant. However, the advent of the train transformed the tunnel's future: in September 1865 it was bought by the East London Railway Company for £200,000. Fortuitously, the height of the tunnel, intended to be sufficient for a carriage and its driver and horses, was also sufficient for underground trains to use. The Thames Tunnel became part of the East London Line, but following improvement works in the 1990s the tunnel now forms part of the London Overground. It is a Grade II* listed structure.

The success of the tunnel-boring venture, in the face of much hostility and pessimism, led to a number of other projects in England – another tunnel under the Thames (the Tower Subway, in 1869) and tunnels under the River Severn and under the River Mersey (both opened in 1886). But all of these projects came about after Marc Brunel had died. His health had deteriorated severely during the construction period and he never accepted any further commissions. In 1845 he suffered a severe stroke which left him significantly paralysed down his right side. He died on 12 December 1849, at the age of 80, and was buried in Kensal Green Cemetery in London. Two others in the family were also buried in the same plot – his widow Sophia in January 1855, and their son, the remarkable Isambard Kingdom Brunel, in September 1859.

In 1814 Marc Isambard Brunel had been elected as a Fellow of the Royal Society and in 1823 had become a member of the Institution of Civil Engineers. In 1839 that institution awarded him their Telford silver medal in recognition of his work on the tunnelling shield. In 1829 he was awarded the French Légion d'honneur, and other awards came from the Royal Academy of Science in Stockholm. He was knighted in March 1841. However, one suspects that his greatest, proudest, moment came when he travelled to Bristol and saw his son launch the SS *Great Britain*. The date: 19 July 1843. One suspects that he would never have minded a single jot that succeeding generations would revere the name of Isambard Kingdom Brunel, whereas his own achievements would be largely forgotten.

An eighteenth-century image of the tunnelling machine used in the Thames Tunnel construction.

Chapter 2

The Heavy Metal Merchants

Above left and above right: A trade token from 1787 showing John Wilkinson, iron master, and a workman holding an item under a trip hammer.

John 'Iron-Mad' Wilkinson, 1728–1808

There can be nothing more frustrating for an inventor than to be ahead of his time; poor Leonardo, coming up with ideas for helicopters and tanks, but doing so hundreds of years before the technology existed to make his pipedream come true. How much more fortunate to be James Watt, who came up with ideas for steam power just as advances in iron-manufacturing technology meant that he could get his hands on high quality iron, in quantity, just when it was needed. And one man more than any other was King Iron, responsible not just for producing around one eighth of the country's entire iron output, but ensuring that it was free from impurities, and therefore not brittle and liable to snap.

That man was John Wilkinson, and it is little wonder that his contemporaries referred to him as 'Iron Mad' Wilkinson. After all, he was obsessed with iron: he made it, he fought his family over it, he built boats out of it, and he chose to be buried in a coffin made from it.

He was born in Cumberland at a place called Little Clifton, and was the eldest son of a potfounder who worked at a local blast furnace. Here, experiments were carried out using coke rather than the more traditional charcoal. The process of producing coke, by burning coal with minimal amounts of oxygen, was first developed by Abraham Darby and involved burning the coal in a huge mound. Only the outer layer came into contact with the air, leaving the coal inside to become carbonised and to convert into coke. The change was significant, not least because the country could not grow coppiced wood fast enough to turn into charcoal in order to meet the demands of the iron industry. Coke meant that there was a constant supply of fuel to fire the blast furnaces, and at a greater heat than ever before. In turn this meant that taller chimneys were needed, and iron production went up in leaps and bounds. But at the time of John Wilkinson's birth in 1728 the production of coke needed refinement. The production method was inefficient and poorly understood, and it fell to John, as an adult, to make substantial improvements both to the coking process and to the generation of much higher temperatures used in the blast furnaces.

In 1745 the 17-year-old John was sent away on a five-year apprenticeship with a Liverpool merchant. That same year saw the birth of his brother William, who was later to compete with him for control of the family business. There was also a sister, Mary, who later married the chemist Joseph Priestley. The Wilkinsons, like Priestley, were Nonconformist Presbyterians, which is why John had been educated at a Dissenters Academy in Kendal.

His apprenticeship complete, John initially stayed behind at Kirby Lonsdale near the edge of the Lake District, when his father moved to Bersham, near Wrexham, to open a new blast furnace. Two years later, in 1755, he entered into partnership with his father in respect of the Bersham works. It was not his only partnership in 1755 – on 17 November he married a local girl called Ann Maudesley. The wealthy daughter of a landowning family in the area, Ann brought much-needed capital into the family. A daughter, Mary, was born the following year and in 1756 the young family moved into rented accommodation a few miles from the Bersham works.

There followed a period of great sadness. John had a middle sibling called Henry but he died at the age of 26. That left John, who was approaching 30, with a very much younger brother, William, not yet into his teens; a wife aged 23, and a daughter less than a year old. His wife Ann died on their first wedding anniversary in 1756, leaving the grieving father to farm out their daughter to be brought up by a local family. He could not have coped in any other way, and at least it meant that he could bury his grief in hard work. The problem was that the Bersham works were proving to be unprofitable, with a limited water supply, coke which did not generate sufficient heat in the blast furnace, and iron which was of poor quality. There certainly was not enough profit in the venture to support both John and his father, leading John to consider other opportunities within the iron-making business.

His opportunity came when he entered into partnership to open a new foundry at Willey in Shropshire. Here he would have learned that the existing lease of nearby foundry premises at New Willey was coming up for renewal. The existing tenant, the Darby's of Coalbrookdale, naturally assumed that they would be carrying on, but must have been outraged when the upstart John Wilkinson took the lease from right under their noses. Litigation between the Coalbrookdale Company and the landlords followed, but Wilkinson and his partners were not directly involved. The forty-two-year lease gave the new tenants ample opportunity to build new and improved furnaces. Using the dowry from his late wife, and in partnership with business partners from Shrewsbury and Bristol, Wilkinson did exactly that. He also took on a lease, in his own name, for premises at Moreton (12 miles from the new Willey works) and so was able to be an iron-master in his own right. In time he decided to concentrate his efforts on the new Willey works, which were developed into the largest iron foundry in the entire area.

Father, back in Bersham, was training his younger son William in the iron-making business and in 1762 retired from the Bersham venture, leaving it jointly to John and William. There is little doubt that John saw himself as the senior partner, and this was to prove to be a source of much friction in later years.

Their father went off to develop what was known as the Plymouth Ironworks (actually in Merthyr Tydfil in South Wales), and in 1763 John chose to remarry. His new wife, a previously unmarried woman of 40 called Mary, was the sister-in-law of his business partner, Edward Blakeway. A wealthy woman in her own right, she not only became a close companion to John for the rest of their lives, but also proved to be a highly competent administrator as well as a homemaker – and a useful source of finance. She was also to prove to be a good stepmother to John's daughter Mary when the 6-year-old joined the couple at their new home, built by John at considerable expense, called The Lawns. It quickly became the centre of operations for all of John's business interests and was referred to by him as his 'headquarters'.

In 1767 John Wilkinson bought the Manor of Bradley, in Bilston. It was midway between Wolverhampton and Birmingham and was quickly developed into a huge iron-production centre. Among the innovations made by John was the introduction of modified bellows to increase the blast inside the furnace. 'Blast' was used to describe the way in which combustion air was being forced into the furnace at greater than atmospheric pressure. The bellows resulted not just in higher temperatures, but also heat which was both reliable and consistent. This proved to be ideal for the production of high quality cast iron. Soon the Bilston works boasted a number of furnaces together with rolling mills, glass and brick works and a pottery. It was a huge enterprise, and one with which John was associated for the rest of his life.

John was continually seeking to improve efficiency and output. Initial modifications to the way that coke was produced eventually led to an efficient way of burning the coal directly for the furnace, a change which apparently helped to double the output of iron ore. More significantly, John introduced a new and much more satisfactory way of making cannon out of iron. Traditionally this had involved casting a long tube of iron and then boring it out with a rotating cutting tool, but this had caused all sorts of problems: the iron casing tended to vary in thickness, the cutting tool often left irregular surfaces, impurities in the iron caused weaknesses and cannons had a tendency to explode when in use. Wilkinson turned the process on its head: he made the barrel as a solid piece of high-quality iron and then, instead of rotating the cutting tool, held it rigidly in place and rotated the cast-iron barrel around it. The method was patented in 1773. However, the navy saw it as a monopoly and maintained that allowing the patent was against the public interest.

Six years later the patent was therefore set aside, but Wilkinson remained a major player in the production of cannon, in due course patenting a method to make spiral grooves in the cannon barrel so that this would propel the cannon ball more accurately and to a greater distance.

The manufacture of cannon benefited greatly when war with France led to a major rearmament programme. Ironically, this did not prevent John's brother William being recruited by the French to go and live in France and to develop foundry premises at Indret on the River Loire near Nantes. Here the latest iron-making methods were used and in 1779 the first cannon, bored in accordance with the Wilkinson patent, was produced. It marked an important stage in the growth of an export market, leading eventually to William Wilkinson securing a contract from the French government to supply vast quantities of iron piping in which to bring a new water supply over a distance of 40 miles to the French capital. Needless to say, the large quantity of pipes stored on the quayside of English ports led people to assume that the family were exporting cannon to France and there were many accusations of treachery and dishonourable conduct made against them, even though the pipeline contract was expressly sanctioned by the British government.

William had grown rich in France and is estimated to have pocketed some £30,000 in salary during a thirteen-year period up to 1789 – equivalent to several million pounds nowadays. So, when he returned to the Bersham works in 1789, John may have thought that his younger brother would not be too worried about claiming his share of the Bersham profits for the time that he was away. In this he was mistaken and when John refused to pay up a lengthy period of litigation followed.

While William was away John had developed a hugely important connection with the partnership of Boulton & Watt. When James Watt had developed his ideas for steam power he was held back by difficulties in producing iron cylinders for the engine. Wilkinson came up with a means of boring out the cylinders – a modification of the cannon-boring method. The result was just what Watt was looking for, with cylinders no longer liable to leak and explode. Wilkinson was given an exclusive contract for the production of all future Boulton & Watt machines.

Wilkinson could see other practical uses for the new steam engines, not just for pumping water out of mines. He saw their future in driving blowing machines in the foundries and for powering forge hammers and rolling mills. He went on to install the first rotary engine at his iron works in Bradley in 1783. Eight years earlier he had been one of the leading lights in the proposal to build an iron bridge across the River Severn, near Broseley. He may not have got the contract to build the actual bridge – that went to Abraham Darby III – but his involvement in getting the plan pushed through parliament and in raising public support was critical to the success of the venture. Iron Bridge marked a milestone for the use of iron and from then on there was no looking back, with iron being used in a whole range of structures. Wilkinson developed a close working relationship with Thomas Telford and provided the iron for the arches and waterbed for the Pontcysyllte Aqueduct. He designed and made iron barges, and in 1792 he bought an estate at Brymbo Hall near Bersham in Denbighshire. Soon, an iron foundry was constructed and the Brymbo site became associated with iron and steel production until the factory finally closed in 1990.

This was not the limit of John Wilkinson's investment in metal ores. He bought shares in copper mines in Cornwall and Anglesey; he also purchased a number of under-performing lead mines and installed new steam pumps, enabling those mines to be brought back into full production.

Throughout the 1790s he became increasingly eccentric. His second wife, Mary, was considered to be past childbearing age when they had married and his only daughter, Mary, had died in childbirth in 1786, leaving him without an heir. In an age where this was certainly not 'the done thing' for businessmen, he took a mistress – a servant girl at Brymbo called Ann Lewis. It is far from clear whether this was done against the wishes of his wife Mary – indeed she may have approved of the arrangement which resulted in the birth of a son and two daughters. The first child, a daughter called Mary Ann, was born in 1802 when John was 74. Another daughter, clearly not the son John wanted, was called Johnina when she was born in 1805. The following year his mistress was at last delivered of a boy, named John. Wilkinson had his son and heir at last, albeit not legitimate. Intriguingly Mrs Wilkinson (Mary) was still alive: she died two months afterwards.

Following the birth of his son, John applied for a coat of arms and in due course royal consent was obtained for the children to assume the name of Wilkinson and the arms were eventually granted to them. A priority for John was to ensure that his mistress would be adequately provided for after his death and that trust funds for the three children would make certain that they were brought up in financial security. He was anxious to make absolutely certain that they would inherit a business which he took for granted would continue long after his death. Unfortunately, his choice of executors and trustees made this assumption somewhat unrealistic.

John died on 14 July 1808, leaving an estate worth more than £9 million in today's money. His crystal ball would not have told him that litigation, commenced by his nephew, would drag on for years and years, until the inheritance intended for his children was largely dissipated in legal fees. The legal claim in the Court of Chancery wended its way right up to the House of Lords, and by 1828 it was clear that the fees had considerably exceeded the value of the estate.

The eccentric John Wilkinson had prepared well for his actual funeral, having already designed and made the iron coffin in which he was to be laid to rest. An iron obelisk was ready to be erected by the graveside at Cumbria's Lindale-in-Cartmel, but the journey from Bradley, where John died, to his Lake District graveside was not an easy one. The journey by road took four days. A shortcut across Morecambe Bay was chosen, but the incoming tide forced the funeral party to abandon the gun-carriage on which the coffin was being carried. The coffin was found stranded on rocks the next day, and was rescued and carried on to its destination at Lindale.

There it was found that the wooden coffin, inside a lead coffin, was too large to fit inside the outer coffin made of iron. The corpse had to be left by the graveside for some days before an even larger iron coffin could be made. Then it was found that the enlarged coffin was too large to fit in the hole which had been hollowed out for it in the limestone rock below the obelisk. More delays followed, while the corpse remained above ground level. Eventually the coffin was lowered, the obelisk finished off, and it was assumed that the corpse would now lie in peace, undisturbed. Wrong! Twenty years later, John's executors were forced to liquidate assets to pay for the litigation and had to sell the house adjoining the site of the grave. The buyers didn't want a body in the garden, however illustrious and however securely interred. The coffin was reported to have been exhumed and may well have been reburied at St Paul's Church in Lindale.

In his lifetime, John Wilkinson had been a titan in the world of iron production. He had ridden roughshod over legal niceties, being on the losing side of litigation not just with his younger brother William, but also with the firm of Boulton & Watt who objected to his use of 'pirate' steam engines. Despite his close working relationship with that company, Wilkinson had not always been keen to pay the royalties which were due; after his death his entire estate was broken up within a comparatively short period of time, largely due to the litigation and mismanagement of his trustees. Within a generation, almost nothing was left of a sprawling industrial empire.

But the fact remains: without Wilkinson's iron, without his tube-boring inventions, James Watt would not have been able to bring his steam engines to the market place in anything like the time-frame which he achieved. Wilkinson was an essential ingredient, and it is unfair to his memory that his contribution is so utterly neglected.

Thomas Lombe, 1685–1739 and John Lombe, 1693–1722

Most schoolchildren studying eighteenth-century history learn about Richard Arkwright and would know that he invented the spinning frame and a rotary carding engine, and was known after his lifetime as the 'father of the modern industrial factory system'. They learn how he was knighted, made High Sheriff, showered with honours, and died leaving an industrial empire – and half a million pounds – in 1792. What this rather overlooks is that most of his wealth and fame was built upon other people's ideas. Most of the patents he took out in his lifetime were overturned, but in many cases the damage had already been done. The 'little men' who made the discoveries were never wealthy enough to fight their corner through the courts. As mentioned in the Preface, we have the situation where Thomas Highs, who invented the spinning frame for cotton, died in poverty in 1803 after relying on charitable donations to support him in the last dozen or so years of his life. Credit for his inventions was eagerly taken by others.

Over the years, assertions have been made that Arkwright was the first to mechanise the production of cloth, but this disregards the fact that machinery for spinning silk had been introduced to Britain many years before. Not only that, but the silk process involved the first water-driven mill, at Derby, on the River Derwent. The contribution of two brothers, John and Thomas Lombe, deserves to be remembered, because theirs was the blueprint followed by many subsequent factory owners, including Arkwright. Not all of their influences were positive – factory conditions were appalling right from the start, with visitors noting the noise, the smell, and the anti-social hours.

The Lombe story is one of industrial espionage, experimentation and allegations of murder. It starts in 1685 with the birth of Thomas Lombe to Henry Lombe, a Norwich weaver, and his first wife. Henry married a second time, and Thomas had a younger half-brother, John. After their father died in around 1695, John was brought up by his mother. By then the growing silk-stocking trade had moved from London and was centred in the Midlands, especially around Derby. The Lombe brothers, aided by a cousin William Lombe, decided to build a watermill on the Derwent to drive the machinery enabling the silk to be made into yarn for weaving. It was not the first attempt at a water-powered silk mill, Thomas Cotchett had tried to build a similar structure in around 1702 using Dutch machinery, but unlike Cotchett's venture, the Lombe mill became hugely successful.

The problem was that the silk production process was a closely guarded secret. Silk had been produced in Italy for several hundred years, and the actual method of 'throwing' the silk and then twisting it into a useable yarn remained in Italy, with disclosure of the method used being punishable by death. The process involved two separate machines, one called a *filatoio*, which was a throwing machine, and another called a *torcitoio*, which was designed to wind the thread onto bobbins. Drawings of neither the *torcitoio* nor the *filatoio* had ever been seen outside Italy, so in 1715 John, then aged around 20, was allegedly sent by Thomas to Italy to try and find out how the machines operated. He is said to have secured employment at a factory in Piedmont where the Italian silk-making industry was based; he would creep back into the factory at night and, by candlelight, take accurate measurements of the machinery and draw the various wheels and spindles which were used in the manufacturing process. These diagrams were then smuggled back to England inside bales of silk which were being imported into England by Thomas. It sounds a nice story, and it is embellished by the idea that he was detected and had to flee for his life, notebooks in hand.

Apparently, he returned to Britain along with a couple of Italian colleagues who were happy to throw in their lot with the Englishman, and together they produced plans for the factory machinery. The same story goes on to suggest that the Italians were so incensed when news got out that they sent a woman to England to befriend John and that, having gained his confidence, this woman administered a slow-working poison over a number of years. Whatever the truth of this (and the story only emerged many years later), young John was ill for quite some time before dying at the age of 29. His funeral was a grand affair and one source states that:

> *exclusive of all the gentlemen who attended, all the people concerned in the works were invited. The procession marched in pairs, and extended the full length of Full Street, the Market Place and Iron Gate, so that when the corpse entered All Saints at St Mary's Gate, the last couple left the house of the deceased at the corner of Silk Mill Lane.*

The huge procession carried flambeaux and candles, and demonstrated the importance which the town accorded to a man who had helped to bring work and prosperity to the community. The church at All Saints is now Derby Cathedral, but no trace of the actual grave remains. When John died he left his share in the business to his cousin William, but apparently William suffered from severe depression and eventually shot himself, leaving Thomas Lombe as sole proprietor of the business.

Back in 1718, Thomas had obtained British patent No. 422 for:

A New Invention of Three Sorts of Engines never before made or used in Great Britaine, One to Wind the Finest Raw Silk, Another to Spin, and the Other to Twist the Finest Italian Raw Silk into Organzine in great Perfection, which was never before done in this Kingdom.

Organzine was the name for the raw silk thread used in weaving. It is by no means certain that Thomas relied entirely on his brother's clandestine efforts at espionage; he may simply have bought a copy of an Italian book published a century earlier giving many of the details of the process. Whatever method was used, the result was an impressive factory, five storeys high, with an undershot watermill drawing water from the Derwent to power the *torcitoio* and *filatoio* machines. Construction cost a whopping £30,000. The factory was brick-built with a height of some 17 metres, topped off with a shallow roof. Water flowed under the building though a series of arches and turned a vertical shaft going up through the first two floors, where the silk was 'thrown'. Power was then diverted to a series of horizontal shafts running the entire length of the factory – over 30 metres long, where the top three floors housed the winding machines.

One of the problems faced by the Lombe brothers was that the silk could only be worked if the temperature and humidity were high. In sunny Italy this had been no problem, but in the gloom and cold of an English factory situated in Derby, the remedy involved heating the entire premises. The warmed air then had to be circulated evenly throughout the factory, and a report from 1732 suggests that this involved a steam engine to pump the air.

The original patent was valid for fourteen years and when it expired in 1732, Thomas Lombe petitioned parliament for an extension. His petition pointed to the great expense involved in training craftsmen from scratch and in introducing such innovative machinery into the country. He was also able to point to the fact that since the factory had started, the cost of organzine, the basic silk thread, had dropped significantly. But there was opposition to the patent being extended, not least from other branches of the fabric-making industry. Cotton and worsted spinners could see advantages within their own trades if they were able to adapt the machines used by Lombe. In the end parliament chucked out the petition, but awarded Thomas Lombe £14,000 in recognition of his efforts.

More workmen were taken on as the factory prospered, until 300 were employed at any given time. Conditions of work were not good, as is apparent from a book written by William Hutton some years later. His *History of Derby*, published in 1791, gives details of his life in the factory. He had been apprenticed as a young boy at the mill, and recalls being made to wear iron raisers, called pattens, on his feet, in order to give him the extra height needed to access the machinery. The job of knotting the silk ends together was done by children, each one in charge of monitoring between twenty and sixty threads. Failure to knot broken ends quickly enough to avoid having to stop the machinery led to a severe beating. Meanwhile, careless fingers must have resulted in many instances of mutilation and injury, and Hutton loathed the place, having to get up at five in the morning and face corporal punishment for the slightest of misdemeanours. He was surrounded by people whom he regarded as 'the most rude and vulgar of the human race, never taught by nature, nor ever wishing to be taught.'

Thomas Lombe went on to achieve high public office, being made Sheriff of London in 1727. He was knighted in July 1727 and when he died in 1732 he was the possessor of a fortune of some £120,000, which he left to his widow and two daughters. His executors were requested to reward the principal servants at the Derby enterprise to the tune of £500 or £600, as his widow should deem appropriate. The mill was sold as a going concern and continued to manufacture spun silk until 1890. After 1910, when the premises were partly destroyed by fire, the mill fell into disuse but has recently been used to house Derby's industrial museum.

Thomas, aided by his brother John, left an enduring legacy. Numerous other mills were opened along similar lines, helping to make Derby the centre of the silk industry. The factory was the first silk mill in the country to be powered by water – indeed the first water-powered factory in the world – and became the precursor of many later industrial centres. Unwittingly or otherwise, Arkwright followed where Lombe led. Outside of Derby, few are familiar with the Lombe name, or are able to appreciate the significance of the brothers' achievements. There is, however, a street in Derby named after them, and a bas relief showing John's profile on one of the city bridges. It is a story which has it all – industrial espionage, murder, suicide – and while many of the aspects of the story are fanciful or heavily embroidered, they do reveal much about the earliest days of what was to become the Industrial Revolution.

Henry Maudslay, 1771–1831

As the Industrial Revolution got underway there was one thing which the country's pioneering engineers wanted, and which had previously only been found in workshops making individual scientific instruments: precision machine tools. What industry wanted was the ability to replicate parts, over and over again. Increasingly, those pioneers turned to one man, Henry Maudslay, to come up with the quite superb craftsmanship which 'held the Industrial Revolution together'. In its most literal sense, Maudslay did this by making the nuts and bolts which heralded mass production. Before Maudslay, nuts and bolts were rarely used – because they had to be made to fit individually. Parts were therefore not interchangeable, and each individual nut and bolt had to be hand-finished by craftsmen relying on the human eye. Maudslay transformed this by producing taps and dies designed to make absolutely standard parts. Screws, which had previously been little-used, could be churned out by the thousand, giving industry the accuracy it needed in order to introduce standardisation and mass production. The skills which had once been the preserve of the craftsman were being replaced by the machine, and Maudslay did so using tools of his own design, operating to an accuracy of one ten-thousandth of an inch. Small wonder that Maudslay features in the stories of so many other inventors of the age. His talents criss-cross the achievements of many of the great inventors of the day, yet he can hardly be said to have had an auspicious start in life.

Maudsley was born in August 1771, the fifth of seven children. His father had been a wheelwright in the Royal Engineers, but had taken a job at Woolwich Arsenal after being wounded in action. Father died in 1780 and when he was 12 years old Henry Maudslay got a job at the arsenal working as a 'powder monkey' – in other words, filling cartridges with gunpowder. After a couple of years he moved on to working in the carpentry shop, and from there to the blacksmith's forge where he showed considerable aptitude working with iron. His skill attracted the attention of the inventor and engineer Joseph Bramah. Here was a man who had not only invented an early form of flush toilet, but had also recently come up with an 'unpickable lock'. The Bramah lock was a superbly engineered padlock, but Bramah needed someone who could make the machinery needed to manufacture the lock on a commercial basis. Impressed by Maudslay's aptitude, Bramah employed the 18-year-old Maudslay at his workshop premises in Denmark Street in the London ward of St Giles.

Maudslay not only designed the machinery, but persuaded Bramah to put the lock in his shop window with a challenge of 200 guineas for anyone who could open it. The challenge went unmet for nearly half a century – and then, in 1850, it took the American locksmith A.C. Smith some fifty-one hours, spread over a sixteen-day period, to open the darned thing. More significantly, Maudslay was able to engineer the lock sufficiently cheaply to make it a commercial success.

Bramah had been working on another new invention, a hydraulic press. He was having difficulty sealing the pressure cylinder around the piston rod but Maudslay came up with a solution: a self-tightening leather cup-washer. Problem solved. Bramah was so impressed that he made Maudslay, then aged 19, manager of the engineering works. All seemed rosy, and for eight years Maudslay worked for Bramah, including experimenting with various improvements to industrial lathes. In 1797 he had the temerity to ask for a pay rise, was declined, and therefore left to set up his own business. The work with lathes, capable of churning out identical items, continued. Specific lathe components, such as the slide rest, and a lead-screw powered by a pair of changeable gears, had been proposed by others, but the Maudslay lathe combined all these components to make a lathe which was far superior to anything previously seen. James Nasmyth, a former apprentice of Maudslay who went on to invent the steam hammer, described the significance of Maudslay's slide lathe as follows:

> *Its influence in improving and extending the use of machinery has been as great as that produced by the improvement of the steam engine in respect to perfecting manufactures, and extending commerce.*

The eye and steady hand of the previous generation of machine operators had been rendered obsolete by precision engineering. And to ensure that precision, Maudslay developed the micrometer screw, capable of testing minute measurements throughout the factory. The micrometer became the ultimate arbiter, known as 'the Lord Chancellor', in deciding whether work was being carried out with sufficient accuracy.

But Maudslay was no nit-picking pedant; he was a large jovial man who inspired his apprentices. In many ways it was his influence on his apprentices which became his biggest legacy. His factory became a centre of excellence to which all aspiring engineers sought admission. If you were a Maudslay Man you were marked for the top! He inspired and motivated them, drumming in the maxims by which he worked. These were intended to encourage clear planning and a dedication to simplifying the process. 'First get a clear notion of what you desire to accomplish, and then you will succeed in doing it', was one maxim. Another was: 'When you want to go from London to Greenwich don't go via Inverness'. Simplicity was paramount, and who can argue with his admonition: 'Remember the get-at-ability of parts. If we go on as some mechanics are doing, we shall soon be boiling our eggs with a chronometer.'

In 1800 Maudslay had moved to larger premises in Margaret Street, Cavendish Square, but within ten years had expanded his operation to the stage where he had a workforce of eighty men and was forced to move to still larger premises in Lambeth, just off Westminster Bridge Road. Here he came to the attention of Marc Brunel who, as mentioned earlier, was looking for someone capable of making the machines needed to make his pulley blocks. Together they commenced production at the purpose-built Portsmouth Block Mills. The pulleys they made were all manufactured to the same precise size and specification, in a demonstration of mass-production which became a blueprint for so many subsequent factory operations.

In 1791 Maudslay had married Sarah Tindel, who had been working as Bramah's housemaid. They had four sons together. Thomas Henry, the eldest, and Joseph, the youngest, and both went on to join their father's engineering business. Another son, William, became a civil engineer and was one of the founders of the Institution of Civil Engineers.

Maudslay turned his attention to marine engineering and his first marine engine, of 17 horsepower, was installed on a Thames steamer named the *Richmond*. A commission from the Royal Navy followed and in 1823 *Lightning*, was launched, to become the navy's first steam-powered ship. Rapid improvements meant that within four years, a Maudslay engine generating 400 horsepower was being installed in HMS *Dee*.

Joseph Maudslay was taken into partnership with his father and quickly developed the marine business. The firm became inextricably linked with the success of Isambard Kingdom Brunel, producing a massive 750 horsepower engine for the SS *Great Western*. By 1850 some 200 steam vessels had been sold, and the firm went on to develop the earliest screw-propulsion units for ships. The Maudslay engineering works went on to become one of the most significant factories in the entire country.

Henry Maudslay's contribution to the success of the Thames Tunnel has already been mentioned. It was his firm which manufactured the unique tunnelling shield, and also made the pumps which kept the tunnel dry. Maudslay never lived to see the tunnel completed. In 1831 he caught a chill crossing the English Channel and died a month later on 15 February. He was buried in St Mary Magdalen Church in Woolwich.

Maudslay's range of inventions was impressive; somewhere along the way he made flour- and sawmills, made precision machinery for minting coins, and produced steam engines. But his greatest legacy was in the way he inspired others and established standards that became the industry norm. He really was an extraordinary man, and his achievements are up there with the very greatest of the Industrial Revolution.

The Lombe factory at Derby.

Chapter 3

A Pair of Lunaticks

The golden trio of Boulton, Watt and Murdoch.

Quite rightly, the Lunar Society, originally known as the Lunar Circle, has been regarded as the crucible of ideas which sparked the Industrial Revolution and pushed Birmingham and the Midlands to the forefront of change. But whereas its members included famous luminaries such as Matthew Boulton, James Watt, Joseph Priestley and Josiah Wedgwood, it also included a number of other members and supporters whose contribution to change has been largely overlooked.

The society had no formal constitution, kept no minutes, and was open (by invitation) to people from all walks of life and from all nationalities. It was a forum for ideas, and as such its contributors included the American Benjamin Franklin, and the Swiss inventor of the oil lamp, Aimé Argand. Its members included natural philosophers, industrialists and intellectuals. This was an era before scientific endeavour had been rigidly divided up into different disciplines. Nowadays it might be hard to find common ground between, say, an astro-physicist and a marine biologist, but back in the second-half of the eighteenth century it was perfectly feasible to think that a well-educated person could share in the knowledge of his contemporaries across a whole spectrum. A medical man could challenge a chemist to consider what benefits could follow from a discovery in the laboratory; a geologist might ask an industrialist whether his improvements to machinery could be put to the greater benefit of mankind. The members were acutely aware that they were living in a new environment, one where change was constant and exciting.

Take some of the other members of this somewhat fluid society: Richard Lovell Edgeworth, who apart from fathering twenty-two children, invented a velocipede, a turnip cutter, various chaises – some running on just one wheel, another with four wheels – and a device for calculating land measurement. He came up with an idea for a wooden robotic horse (forerunner of a modern tank); an umbrella for covering haystacks; and numerous other ingenious labour-saving devices. He also developed an early form of telegraphic communication using semaphore and proposed a number of road-building improvements. It can be argued that none of these changed the face of British society, but his ideas were indicative of the range of an enquiring mind.

Take James Keir, a man who studied medicine at Glasgow and went on to take over the management of the Boulton and Watt Soho Manufactory in the late 1770s. Later, he invented an alloy of copper, zinc and iron which could be forged both hot and cold. He developed a chemical works at Tipton which was to become an important factory, manufacturing soap. He was also a geologist, owned a colliery, ran a glassworks, and translated French chemistry books into English.

Take Jonathan Stokes and William Withering, two Lunar Society members whose work on the properties of digitalis led to important advances in the treatment of heart disease. As a group, these members of a remarkable Society led to changes which affected every nook and cranny of Georgian life. And yet there were two members whose fame and recognition is substantially less than they deserved: William Murdoch and Erasmus Darwin.

William Murdoch, 1754–1839

Perhaps more than anyone else, William Murdoch – or William Murdock as he became known in his name's Anglicised format – shows how fame can be so bright that it leaves bystanders in the shade. In this case, James Watt takes all the spotlight, all the fame and all the glory. But go to Birmingham's Broad Street and you will see an impressive gilded statue of three men. It is nicknamed variously the 'The Golden Boys' (after its colour), 'The Carpet Salesmen' (because it looks as if the three men are unrolling a carpet), or 'The Moonstones' (after the fact that the men represented in the statue were all members of the Lunar Society). It is shown at the heading of this chapter. The three men are Matthew Boulton, the great industrialist who helped put Birmingham on the map as the epicentre of the Industrial Revolution; James Watt, inventor of the steam engine; and William Murdoch. Matthew Boulton and James Watt are well-known figures, but the third man is a bit of an enigma. Murdoch seems almost incongruous, as if he doesn't really deserve his spot in the limelight – and yet arguably he was the greatest inventor of them all. Watt was so famous that in 1862, some sixty-three years after his death, the British Association named the basic unit of electrical power after him, and as a result, some two centuries after he died, his name can be found on just about every lightbulb in the world. Asking for a '40-Murdoch bulb' would perhaps be more appropriate – because Murdoch, unlike James Watt, was at least involved in bringing light into people's lives.

His list and range of inventions is staggering – he did not just bring gas lighting to the world; in the 1790s, he also invented a pneumatic tube system for sending messages, as well as making a steam-powered gun. He worked on early paddle-steamer designs and made a number of discoveries in the field of chemistry, in particular regarding analine dyes. Besides working on machine tools he built a prototype self-propelled vehicle – a steam locomotive subsequently developed by others. He made a number of improvements to Watt's engine which were claimed by Watt as his own. The point here is that, in common with modern contracts of employment which deal with intellectual property rights, inventions made by Murdoch while in the employment of Boulton & Watt were regarded as belonging to his employers. Even when he worked for the company on a freelance basis, he was discouraged from taking out patents or developing his ideas into commercially viable inventions. It rather looks as though James Watt in particular was jealous of his protégé's talents, and was perfectly happy to take the credit himself. Further, when Matthew Boulton and James Watt died, to be succeeded by their respective sons, Murdoch found the successors too timid and cautious to try anything new. In short, Murdoch got shafted every which way.

He was born in the Ayrshire village of Old Cumnock in 1754, one of seven children. His father was a miller and millwright, and was married to Anne, whose brother was an agent for the estates belonging to the diarist James Boswell. The connection was probably significant because Boswell had visited the Boulton & Watt factory at Soho in Birmingham in March 1776 and in the following year the 23-year-old William Murdoch set off for the same Soho works to meet the two men. It was a journey he made on foot – a distance of some 300 miles.

According to legend, Murdoch had with him a wooden hat, which he had turned on a lathe – designed to his own specification, and Matthew Boulton was so taken with the titfer – or at least, the story of the lathe – that he offered him a job on the spot. Boulton wrote to Watt later that year, saying 'I think Wm. Murdoch a valuable man and deserves every civility and encouragement.' Within months he had become the company's most trusted pattern maker. He was then quickly put in charge of erecting the actual engines on site – usually by a mine shaft, so that the machine could pump water from the mine, allowing the owner to drive shafts deeper and deeper underground. In this way, the landowner could maximise his profits. The efficiency of the engine – measured by the volume of water it could shift – was critical to Boulton & Watt's charging structure – they didn't just sell the engines, they installed them and then charged the mine owner a percentage based upon the efficiency of each engine. Watt developed the concept of 'horse power' and charged purchasers a fee, over and above the cost of the engine, based upon the savings the mine owner could make by virtue of no longer having to keep and feed the corresponding number of horses.

Murdoch started to make improvements to the Watt design, in order to make the engine installation simpler and quicker. In particular, he modified the gears so that the action of the exhaust shaft could automatically work the steam valve. These variations were generally not subject to prior approval from Watt, who must have had very mixed views about this outstanding engineer who did not necessarily do as he was told, was generally stubborn and awkward to deal with, but who nonetheless proved to be absolutely indispensable. By the autumn of 1769 Murdoch had been sent to Cornwall to oversee the installation of engines throughout the county's tin-mining region. As Boulton commented in 1782:

We want more Murdochs, for of all others he is the most active man and best engine erector I ever saw…When I look at the work done it astonishes me & is entirely owing to the spirit and activity of Murdoch who hath not gone to bed 3 of the nights.

Watt was opposed to any inventions or improvements unless he could see a positive return, in monetary terms. As far as he was concerned, he had come up with an improvement to the basic engine patented by Newcomen in 1712, half-a-century earlier, and now all he wanted to do was sell as many units as possible. Murdoch, on the other hand, was always looking for greater efficiency, and it was his idea, patented by Watt in October 1781, to develop what became known as the 'sun and planet gear'. This was a device for 'producing a continued Rotative or Circular Motion round an Axis or Centre, and thereby to give Motion to the Wheels of Mills or other Machines', and was described by Murdoch in a letter to Watt which pre-dates the patent by several months. There are a number of other inventions claimed by Watt, which in all probability result from Murdoch's own genius and there is a suspicion that Watt's personal papers may subsequently have been 'doctored' by his sons in order to conceal the true extent of Murdoch's involvement. Certainly, it was not until 1799 that Murdoch patented a development in his own name – in this case the steam wheel, precursor of the steam turbine, offering a simpler and more efficient way of harnessing the power of the steam to turn the wheel.

Murdoch was a keen fan of experimenting with compressed air – experiments which led to the invention of the pneumatic air-messaging system used in shops for many years, and to a bell system operated by compressed air. Other inventions saw the steam-powered gun and cannon make an appearance and the (apparently accidental) discovery of an iron cement. This involved mixing ammonium chloride (known as sal amoniac) and iron filings. The story goes that these two components had mixed themselves inside Murdoch's tool bag – and had made a hard, durable cement which was to prove invaluable in creating a strong seal around steam engine joints.

The range of his interests was astonishing. In chemistry, he developed new dyes (the forerunner of modern aniline dyes), and a method of treating ships timbers with 'a composition for preserving the bottoms of all kinds of vessels and all wood required to be immersed in water, from worms, weeds, barnacles, and every other foulness which usually does or may adhere thereto'. He also discovered a way of making isinglass – used in the production of beer as part of the fining process, using dried cod rather than the expensively imported sturgeon from Russia, as had previously been the case. No wonder the London brewers paid him £2,000 for *that* discovery....

A brilliant and tireless inventor, Murdoch started to experiment with his ideas about a steam-driven carriage. Watt was horrified and saw no practical advantage in the idea, writing to Boulton that he wished Murdoch would stop chasing shadows and 'could be brought to do as we do, to mind the business in hand'. But the idea kept gnawing away at Murdoch; he made a number of scale models of his steam carriage in the period from 1782 to 1785. A neighbour in Cornwall wrote to Watt saying:

> *It is no less than drawing carriages upon the road with steam engines ... he says that what he proposes, is different from anything you ever thought of, and that he is positively certain of it answering and that there is a great deal of money to be made by it.*

Boulton himself saw the model carriage and knew that it could work – and knew that Murdoch would not easily be fobbed off. Indeed, Murdoch was on his way from Cornwall via Exeter in order to go to London to take out a patent, when Boulton caught up with him. Boulton managed to talk his man out of the scheme, and to head back to the mines in Cornwall. Writing to his partner James Watt on 2 September 1795 Boulton said:

> *He [Murdoch] said He was going to London to get Men but I soon found he was going there with his Steam Carg to shew it & to take out a patent.... However, I prevailed upon him readily to return to Cornwall by the next days diligence & he accordingly arivd here this day at noon, since which he hath unpacked his Carg & made Travil a Mile or two in Rivers's great room in a Circle making it carry the fire Shovel, poker & tongs.*

The demonstration took place in the Great Rivers Room at The King's Head Hotel in Truro. Boulton went on to explain to Watt that Murdoch,

> *proposes to catch most of the condensed Steam by making it strike against broad Copper plates & the condensed part trickling down may be caught and returned into its Boiler or other reservoir. This may do some good in rain or frosty weather & he proposes to have different sized revolvers to apply at every hill & every vale according to their angle with ye Horizon… I verely believe he would sooner give up all his cornish business & interest than be deprived of carrying the thing into execution.*

Watt had no intention of dabbling in steam locomotion; he was aware that this would have necessitated using a high-pressure steam cylinder and did not think that this could be done safely. But to head off trouble, and in the hope that Murdoch could be persuaded to go back down the mines to install more Boulton & Watt engines, Watt agreed to tag on a steam carriage to his own patent application. He wrote: 'I have given such descriptions of engines for wheel carriages as I could do in the time and space I could allow myself; but it is very defective and can only serve to keep other people from similar patents.' In other words, he was happy to block anyone else from developing the idea, but had no intention of spending any time or money expanding it into anything practical.

It was left to Murdoch to experiment with various models – and possibly even a full-size version – of his engine and there are various unsubstantiated reports of a horseless carriage seen around Redruth causing consternation among the locals. Over time, Murdoch's ideas 'ran out of steam', and it was left to his immediate neighbour in Redruth, a man called Richard Trevithick, to develop the invention into a practical reality. One can only wonder what Murdoch might have achieved if Watt had had the foresight and courage to back his brilliant engineer.

Two other inventions associated with steam power deserve to be credited to Murdoch – the D-slide valve and the oscillating cylinder. The valve was patented in 1799, despite Watt's initial opposition. He really does come across as a Doubting Thomas, interested only in the immediate financial benefits of each development Murdoch came up with. In this case, Watt admitted in old age that initially he had 'set his face against it [but] now am satisfied it is an improvement after all as … it has rendered the engine much simpler and so there are fewer parts to go wrong'. The D-slide valve was to remain in use as the main type of valve in steam engines for most of the following century.

The oscillating cylinder was an example of how good Murdoch was at lateral thinking; he was looking at ways a paddle steamer could be operated by steam power.

James Watt junior had purchased the *Caledonia*, intending to convert her to steam power, and Murdoch had been asked to head up the marine division of Boulton & Watt. His challenge was to adapt the ship and install two 14 horsepower engines to drive the paddles. The problem with the existing beam engines was that they took up a lot of space, were immensely heavy and had a high centre of gravity, making them unsuitable for use at sea. Murdoch turned the whole cylinder through 90 degrees, did away with the beam, and came up with a solution which enabled trials to be carried out on the *Caledonia*, resulting in the first crossing of the English Channel by a steam ship, some time in 1817. All the work in modifying the vessel, in installing the engines, and in experimenting with the size and depth of paddles, was carried out by Murdoch. The success of his endeavours resulted in the Royal Navy commissioning Boulton & Watt to supply some fifty vessels in the period up until 1830. In that year Murdoch was persuaded to retire from the business – although he continued with his ideas for new gadgets and inventions right up until he died, aged 85, in 1839.

In his private life Murdoch encountered many setbacks. He is believed to have contracted malaria in June 1783 while staying in Cornwall. He was nursed by Anne Paynter, daughter of the local mine owner at Chacewater, where Murdoch had been installing a steam engine. Anne's bedside manner apparently extended to more personal matters, as a result of which she became pregnant – and the couple married by Special Licence in December 1785. Twins were born the following year but both died before their second birthday. A boy, William, was born in 1788 and John was born in May 1790, but Anne died almost immediately after the birth leaving Murdoch to bring up the young family on his own, in a county where antipathy towards outsiders was rife. Worse, the Cornish were no respecters of patents and legal rights, and threatened to take personal action against Murdoch if he dared to complain about some of the attempts to copy his designs and ideas. Later, when he was working on the *Caledonia*, he was often affected by crippling rheumatism and general ill-health. In 1798, he moved from Cornwall to be near the Soho works, where he had been given the job of overseeing the new Boulton & Watt foundry. Under his direction the factory became a model for modern mass production, using compressed air as a motive power for many of the machine tools which Murdoch himself developed. In 1817 he built himself a fine gentleman's residence, called Sycamore, at Handsworth, not far from the new foundry. There he was able to impress visitors with his personal touches – such as doorbells operated by compressed air, and piped gaslight throughout the house.

These passions and inventions speak of a man who achieved remarkable things, for very little credit. But this does not even take into account what was perhaps his greatest and most significant work – the development of gas lighting. Some stories suggest that he was already experimenting with gas, produced by heating coal, when he was a young boy growing up in Scotland. Other tales concern his time in Redruth, and feature Murdoch walking on pitch-dark nights with a bladder filled with coal gas under his arm, the flame shooting forth from a nozzle made out of the end of a smoker's pipe.

What is clear is that from the start of 1792, Murdoch began to experiment with producing gas at his home in Redruth, next door to his foundry. A neighbour described seeing a large retort in the back yard in 1794, and speaks of 'gas-pipes conveying gas from the retort in the little yard to near the ceiling of the room, just over the table. A hole for the pipe was made in the window-frame.' When Murdoch moved back to Birmingham he continued to experiment, and his work caught the attention of George Lee, who owned a cotton factory in Manchester. Murdoch continued with his research, determining the amount of heat needed to be used to produce the maximum amount of gas, working out how to purify it in order to get rid of the noxious odour, and devising a means of storing the gas (the gasometer). All this took some years. Nevertheless, when hostilities with France were brought to a (temporary) end in 1802 with the Treaty of Amiens, Murdoch marked the celebrations by installing gas lights outside the Soho works. This became a local sensation and triggered off a form of tourism just to see the façade of the factory building illuminated.

By 1806 George Lee was able to install the first fifty of what were to become 900 lights in his factory. Suddenly workers could continue production all year round, all day long. Employers were able to introduce shift working, a major innovation, and one which could never have happened but for the factory premises enjoying artificial illumination. In 1808, James Watt Jnr. prepared a paper outlining the discovery, to be delivered to the Royal Society by Sir Joseph Banks. The firm of Boulton & Watt were happy to take the credit but the company failed to see the commercial potential and did nothing to develop the idea. Murdoch was talked out of applying for a patent himself, on the grounds that it was not a commercially viable project. Indeed, Murdoch made no money whatsoever out of the discovery – although he was awarded the Royal Society's prestigious Rumford Medal for his trouble. It speaks volumes for the lack of foresight and business acumen on the part of the sons of Matthew Boulton and James Watt that it was left for others to develop Murdoch's ideas for entire streets, factories, and towns to be lit by gas light. During the period to 1812, Boulton & Watt vociferously and successfully lobbied parliament to prevent the National Heat and Light Company being granted a charter to develop gas lighting, but they did little or nothing themselves to progress matters and indeed abandoned the gas production business altogether in 1814. It was a short-sighted decision because within a matter of a few years major streets in cities and towns the length and breadth of the country were being lit by gas lights.

Murdoch missed out on a fortune – but contributed to a massive change in the way everyday life was lived. Darkness would never be the same again…

Erasmus Darwin, 1731–1802

Twenty years before he wrote his excellent *Erasmus Darwin – a life of unequalled achievement*, the biographer Desmond King-Hele wrote down a list of the topics which had captured the imagination of his subject. They reveal an extraordinary breadth of interest and knowledge, and in alphabetical order, it is worth repeating:

> *Adiabatic expansion, aesthetics, afforestation, air travel, animal camouflage, artesian wells, an artificial bird, aurorae, balloon flying, biological adaptation, biological pest control, canal lifts, carriage springs, carriage steering, cataract surgery, centrifugation, climate control, clouds, cold and warm fronts, compressed-air actuators, copying machines, cosmology, educational reform, electrical machines, electro-chemistry, electro-therapy, evolution, exercise for children, feminism, fertilizers, formation of coal, geological strata, hereditary diseases, hydrogen engine, ideal gas law, individuality of buds, language, liberation of slaves, limestone deposits, manures, mental illness, microscopy, mimicry, moon's origin, nerve impulses, night airglow, ocula spectra, oil drilling, oil lamps, organic happiness, origin of life, outer atmosphere, oxygenation of blood, phosphorous, photo-synthesis, plant nutrients, Portland Vase, psychology, rocket motors, rotary pumps, science fiction, secular morality, seed-drills, sewage farms, sexual reproduction, speaking machines, squinting, steam carriages, steam turbines, stomata of leaves, struggle for existence, submarines, survival of the fittest, telescopes, temperance, travel of seed, treatment of dropsy, ventilation, water as H2O, water closets, water machines, weather maps, wind gauges, windmills and winds.*

It is an astonishing list of interests and reveals the erudite Erasmus Darwin as being so much more than a country doctor – albeit one who wrote books about plants and vegetables!

Erasmus Darwin was born in 1731 in a village near Nottingham. Father had qualified as a lawyer – but practised medicine – and Erasmus was one of seven children. Educated at Chesterfield Grammar school, he then went to Cambridge University (St John's College) before attending the University of Edinburgh Medical School. A life in London had no appeal for him, and he chose to become a country physician, first in Nottingham and then in Lichfield. As a doctor he became pre-eminent throughout the country, and even turned down the offer of an appointment as Royal Physician to George III. He married twice, fathered at least fourteen children (legitimate and otherwise), and prospered despite a somewhat unattractive face and physique. Contemporaries referred to him as being corpulent, clumsy and frequently badly dressed.

He was a founder-member of what became the Lunar Society and a close friend of many of its members and guests. He helped inspire, challenge and encourage them, and discussed improvements and applications for new discoveries. He was also a member of the influential Derby Philosophical Society and formed the Lichfield Botanical Society. The latter helped him translate the works of the Swedish naturalist Linnaeus from Latin into English, the result being published in two parts as *A System of Vegetables* between 1783 and 1785, and as *The Families of Plants* in 1787. In doing so, Darwin introduced many new words into the English language in order to describe different plants and their various parts and distinguishing features. His main scientific publication was perhaps *Zoonomia*, which came out between 1794 and 1796.

Above all, Darwin was keen to demonstrate his own credentials as an inventor. The list of his inventions is eclectic to say the least. They include:

A horizontal windmill, which he designed for Josiah Wedgwood and which was used for many years as a flint-mill to grind colours for use at his Etruria Works.

A steering mechanism for his carriage, nowadays described as the Ackerman linkage. He proposed this in 1759 and it would be adopted by motor vehicles 130 years later. The fact that Rudolph Ackerman held a patent for the idea in the early part of the nineteenth century did not in any way mean that Ackerman invented it. Like all his inventions, Darwin declined to take out any patents in his own name, believing it could harm his reputation as a doctor. In practice, the linkage system which he proposed was used in automobiles right up until the start of the Second World War. He also proposed a number of other improvements, road tested on his own carriages, linked to making them more stable, easier to manoeuvre, and so on.

A speaking machine, involving an artificial larynx made of wood and leather, incorporating a silk ribbon about an inch long and a quarter of an inch wide, against which air was blown via bellows. It caused a sensation wherever it was exhibited.

A canal lift for barges. This was a way of obviating the need for a whole flight of locks on a steep gradient, or of overcoming the problems encountered by lock-builders when a canal was to be linked up to a river passing below it. The idea was described by Darwin as follows:

> *Let a wooden box be constructed so large as to receive a loaded boat. Let the box be joined [to] the end of the upper canal and then the boat be admitted, and the doors of admission secured again. Then the box with the boat in it, being balanced on wheels, or levers, is let down, and becomes part of the inferior lock.*

Later, he suggested that the whole mechanism should simply be counter-balanced by a second identical wooden box, so that the arrangement could be used to lift a boat simultaneously with the one being lowered. This meant considerable savings in energy – and also saved water which would otherwise be wasted if multiple locks had been used. It was an idea put into practice in many situations from 1790 onwards – and lies at the heart of the rotating boat wheel known as the Falkirk Wheel, erected in 2002 and linking the Forth and Clyde Canal with the Union Canal.

An artificial bird with flapping wings operated by a watch spring. This was not as obscure as it sounds; by mimicking the flight of a goose, Darwin was accurately identifying and solving two of the problems associated with flight – the generation of lift and forward thrust, and the provision of sufficient power to give propulsion. It still left the problem of aerodynamic stability, but it remains an important step in the history of aviation, and showed considerable advances over anything which had been designed before.

A copying machine. Darwin first started working on this in 1777, calling it a 'bigrapher'. The text, written out by quill pen, was duplicated via a tube halfway along an arm, 4ft long. Later, Darwin experimented with what he called a 'polygrapher', and, once satisfied that he had perfected the machine, dismantled it and sent it in parts to his friend Charles Greville, along with eighteen pages of instructions. Unfortunately, these proved quite beyond the engineering capabilities of the recipient, and the machine remained in its box indefinitely. Darwin had, however, shown the working machine to James Watt, who was so impressed with it that he promptly started to experiment with his own copying device – in this case using chemicals. It did not produce an instantaneous copy like the Darwin invention, and it meant that the copy was on a flimsy sheet of paper whereas the Darwin duplicate was crisp and sharp, and could use fine quality paper. But Watt was the man who knew how to market the idea, and he gleefully took out his own patent in 1779 and informed Darwin that his machine 'beat your bigrapher hollow'. The machine was a considerable financial success for Watt and he sold 630 of his machines in the first year alone.

The Artesian Well. Darwin explained the underlying principle, whereby water is stored between different strata of rock and emerges under pressure as a spring, which can then be harnessed to provide water for domestic use. Nowadays, much of the water supply throughout southern England uses artesian wells. Darwin was the first to dig a well precisely because he knew from the nearby rock formations that there was bound to be water under his garden, and that it would rise under its own pressure. Other artesian wells had previously been found, by accident, but Darwin set out the 'how, why and where', and set out the principle behind their existence.

His range of interests extended to researching the effects of different gases to reduce infection and to prevent the spread of cancers – work which resulted in the establishment of the Pneumatic Institute at 6 Dory Square, Bristol, in 1799. James Watt designed much of the apparatus used to produce and administer the gases to patients (including 'laughing gas' and carbon dioxide) and many of these techniques and tools are still used in medicine today.

Other ideas were not ready to be tested or put into practice; in 1779 he produced a sketch of a liquid-fuel rocket engine, using hydrogen and oxygen tanks strapped to the side of a combustion chamber. It would be another 100 years before anyone was ready to test that one, by which time of course his ideas for a combustion chamber and expansion nozzle were much modified.

His interests extended to meteorology, resulting in a 1788 paper published in the *Philosophical Transactions* of the Royal Society. It defined the 'adiabatic expansion of gases', and explained the formation of clouds – and it remains the first, and most important, work in this area of physics. It inspired later scientists such as James Joule to 'finish the job' by coming up with the mathematical formula of the adiabatic law – a key concept in thermodynamics.

But perhaps most important of all, Erasmus Darwin laid the foundation stone for the ideas on evolution, the origin of species and the concept of the survival of the fittest proposed in subsequent years by his grandson Charles Darwin. Here is his comment in *Zoonomia*:

Would it be too bold to imagine, that in the great length of time, since the earth began to exist, perhaps millions of ages before the commencement of the history of mankind, would it be too bold to imagine, that all warm-blooded animals have arisen from one living filament .... possessing the faculty of continuing to improve by its own inherent activity, and of delivering down those improvements by generation to its posterity.

After 1771 Erasmus Darwin drove a carriage with a cartouche on the side showing a conch shell and a Latin inscription which translates as 'Everything from shells' – an expression of the belief that all life is derived from a common ancestor – the so-called theory of common descent. And in case this no longer appears to us to be revolutionary, remember that the prevailing view in the eighteenth century stemmed from the assertion by the Irish Archbishop James Ussher of Armagh, that the world was created as a completed form on the night of 23 October 4004 BC. In his book, the world represented 6,000 years of continuity and constancy – whereas

Erasmus Darwin and his conch analogy was arguing that evolution has been going on around us for many millennia. It may have been Charles who found the proof about evolution, but it was his grandfather who helped create the climate in which such ideas could flourish.

Erasmus Darwin died on 18 April 1802, at the age of 71, and is buried at All Saints Church, in Breadsall, just north of Derby. If ever anyone deserved the epithet 'polymath', it was this extraordinary man, and it is a shame that the world apparently does not have room to honour two 'Darwins'. Erasmus will always remain totally over-shadowed by Charles.

Wax image of Erasmus Darwin, artist unknown.

Chapter 4

The Faux Merchants

It has to be said, the Georgians were great at faking things – not in a bad way, but in a way which made mass-produced items affordable to the general public, by using materials which looked like the real thing, but which were in fact … fake. One example would be coade stone – named after Eleanor Coade – which was an artificial stone (actually a form of ceramic) which could be moulded and then carved. By erecting a factory for the production of columns, friezes, fireplaces, chimney pots and so on, Eleanor Coade was able to feed the growing demand for instant gentrification of the fine country houses being built for the newly rich. You wanted a dozen statues of Adonis to line your driveway? You thumbed through the Coade catalogue, chose the design, and a few months later there would be a delivery at your doorstep of twelve identical statues.

Baskerville typeface.

But there were many other products made by industrialists who wanted to mimic the effects of using original and often expensive materials – people who never gave their name to the product and are therefore quickly forgotten. John Baskerville and Henry Clay are two such industrialists, while Christopher Pinchbeck and Thomas Boulsover came up with alloys which copied the characteristics of gold and silver respectively and in doing so reduced the cost of what had always been seen as high-end merchandise.

John Baskerville, 1706–1775

In the case of John Baskerville he is remembered, if at all, for the exquisite typeface which he designed and which is named after him. But printing was a hobby which he came to later in life – after he had made his fortune manufacturing what were termed 'japanned wares'; in other words, goods made to imitate Chinese and Japanese lacquerware. The problem was that the tree used to extract the lacquer in the Far East (*Toxicodendron vernicifluum*, better known as the Chinese Lacquer Tree) was not available in Europe. In the second-half of the 1600s, a way had been found to take a base material, such as wood or paper, and coat it with layer after layer of coloured resin, like shellac. The procedure was described in publications such as Stalker and Parker's *Treatise of Japanning and Varnishing*, which appeared in 1688, and which does little to hint at the dirty, odorous and often hot working conditions endured by the people doing the japanning. The resin was applied in layers to produce a lustrous finish, usually black, achieved by mixing lamp-black into the resin. Stalker and Parker's *Treatise* explained how to get the lamp black:

> *To make lamp black: Being furnished with a lamp that has 3 or 4 spouts, for as many lights and cotton-week [wick] which you may have at the Tallow Chandlers, twisted up so big that it will but just go into the nose of your spouts; for the greater light they make, the greater quantity of black is afforded. Procure a quart of oyl, by the oyl shops rated at 6d., and so much will make black enough to use about a large cabinet. Get a thing to receive your black in, such in shape and substance as you may often see is planted over a candle to keep the flame and smoak from the roof or ceiling of a room. Having placed your weeks [wicks] in their proper apartment, and put in the oyl, fire or light 'em and fix your receiver over them so close, that the flame may almost touch them. After it is continued so the space of half an hour, take off your receiver, and with a feather strike and sweep off all the black on it. Snuff your weeks, and put it on again, but forget not to supply your lamp with oyl, as often as occasion shall require, and when you imagine that more black is stuck to the receiver, do as before directed.*

Different manufacturers used different varnishes. One, known as 'tar varnish' or 'Jewish pitch', involved a mixture of black asphaltum, amber, linseed oil and rosin in turpentine. In order to achieve a higher gloss, this would then be coated with a mixture of copal resin in linseed oil – or with a variety of spirit varnishes. But as each layer was built up the japanners had to resort to frequent stovings – which in turn had a tendency to warp and crack the underlying base material. In time many japanners turned to tinplate as an alternative to a wood or paper base, because this was more resistant to the damage caused by the stoving process. The high glossy black finish was often embellished with gold decorations, or set off with pictures of flowers and country scenes and used in the production of trays, salvers and tea tables – an ideal setting for the tea ceremonies which developed throughout the eighteenth century.

Very often japanning was done in small factory units and during the Georgian period these started to be clustered around towns in the West Midlands, such as Wolverhampton and Bilston. And then John Baskerville appeared on the scene to develop a way of japanning onto a papier mâché base. It produced a strong but lightweight material which did not warp when the resins were being oven-dried, and Baskerville set up in business in 1740 at 22 Moor Street in central Birmingham. Five years later production was moved to workshop premises in the 8-acre grounds of the fine house he built at Easy Hill on the edge of Birmingham, and before long he was supplying the market with a range of high-quality products. He continued to make papier mâché products from that address for the remainder of his life, taking on a succession of apprentices (seven in all) during the period between 1754 and 1765. Baskerville loved flaunting his success, and had a reputation for wearing clothes richly adorned with gold lace. And, to make sure that no one could mistake him, he bought a pair of cream-coloured horses to draw his carriage, which had its doors and side panels made from papier mâché, richly decorated by the master's hand. Here was a man who did not believe in hiding his light under a bushel...

John was born near Kidderminster in 1707, and initially had made a living teaching calligraphy, and carving gravestones. As a 20-year-old he had moved to Birmingham and set up a school in the Bull Ring, where he taught writing and bookkeeping, while still maintaining his work as an engraver. A slate inscribed with the words 'Grave Stones Cut in any of the Hands by John Baskervill, Writing Master', is all that remains of his business. He was in his late thirties when he stumbled across the use of papier mâché as a substrate for lacquer-work – allegedly as a result of following another papier-mâché maker around the city's apothecaries, noting exactly what products were being bought. He ended up producing products which had the appearance of being made of wood, but which were feather-light, durable and with a very even high-gloss finish.

Having amassed a fortune making lacquered papier mâché with his innovative production methods, he turned back to his first love – the printed word. During the 1750s he developed the use of wove paper (as opposed to laid paper). Wove paper, which was used for a smooth white finish, had been invented by James Whatman, and Baskerville was the first person to see its commercial possibilities. He also experimented with using clearer, more lustrous inks, and developed a system for drying the ink quickly and evenly – preventing it from being soaked into the paper and instead giving a consistent and clear finish. He also brought about changes to the way that the metal type was cast, making the printed word appear really crisp. He really was a pioneer in the field of printmaking, design and book production, and his name quickly became a byword for quality.

All these developments were reflected in the production of his first book in 1757, a superb edition of works by Virgil. The care taken by Baskerville was astonishing – the production of that one volume took three years, but the result was so impressive that Baskerville was appointed printer to Cambridge University. Shortly afterwards he started work on the production of a remarkable folio edition of the Bible, which was finally published in 1763. The care taken was all the more surprising when you consider that Baskerville was an atheist – not a closet atheist, but a highly prominent and vociferous atheist who was not afraid to demonstrate his rejection of Christian doctrines. This even extended to his willingness to live with someone else's wife, the long-suffering Sarah Eaves. Sarah was originally a servant girl and was still married to a Mr Eaves. She had two children by her husband, but John Baskerville treated them as his own, and brazenly set up home with Sarah for some twenty years. It is thought that the couple eventually did marry, after the death of Mr Eaves, but to eighteenth-century moralists, 'living in sin' for two decades with an adulterous woman was not generally acceptable.

John Wilkes said that Baskerville shocked him with his openly atheistic stance and that he was 'a terrible infidel' – which makes it all the more amazing that during his life Baskerville printed three Bibles, nine common prayers, two psalm-books, and two Greek testaments. When he started as a printer he announced: 'It is not my desire to print many books; but such only as are books of consequence, of intrinsic merit, or established reputation.' These books included works by Milton, Addison, Congreve, Shaftesbury, Virgil, Juvenal, Horace, the Italian renaissance poet Ludovico Ariosto and a number of other classical Italian authors.

As a printer he was able to direct John Handy, his punch-maker, to design and produce a new and exceptionally clear and simple typeface. It so impressed Benjamin Franklin (a fellow printer), that when he returned to the newly created United States of America, Franklin directed that federal government documents were to be printed using the Baskerville typeface. Baskerville was elected a member to the Royal Society of Arts, and became an associate of many of the members of the Lunar Society. As a result of this sort of networking he became an important influencer – a major player in Birmingham's industrial scene. In effect he became mentor to the young Matthew Boulton, encouraging him in his early endeavours and, in 1767, lending him the not insignificant sum of £1,470. Boulton, of course, went on to fame and fortune as one of the great architects of the Industrial Revolution, but it is worth remembering that he only achieved that pinnacle because of the support and encouragement given to him by others in his early years.

Baskerville's typefaces mark a high point in the transition between Old Style and Modern type design; they are beautifully cut, and although they went out of fashion, they were subsequently picked up in the twentieth century by type foundries such as Linotype and Monotype. Baskerville helped establish Birmingham as the leading city for print and publishing outside of London, with a reputation as a leader in design. He may have made his money by making cheap imitations of Far Eastern handicrafts, but he spent his money in becoming one of the finest printers of the Age. And if we think of elegance as being the mark of the Georgian era, it is worth remembering that elegance does not simply consist of a neoclassical teapot, or an Adam fireplace or a fine façade designed by William Chambers – it is also defined by the beauty of the printed page.

Baskerville died in January 1775 at his Easy Hill home, having left very specific instructions that his mortal remains were not to be buried in consecrated land, but in a vault which he had created in an old mill building. As he said: 'Doubtless to many [this] may appear a whim – perhaps it is so – but it is a whim for many years resolved upon, as I have a hearty contempt for all superstition [and] the farce of a consecrated ground….'

In practice, his coffin was to have a somewhat nomadic existence – Easy Hill was burnt down in the Birmingham Riots of 1791, and the mausoleum was knocked down when a canal was rerouted across the site. The lead-lined coffin was moved to a warehouse in 1821 where is was used as a workbench and later became something of a tourist attraction as people asked to see the corpse. Originally in a good state of preservation, this constant exposure to the air caused rapid deterioration to the body. Finally, the odorous corpse was secreted in a family vault belonging to a local publisher. Years later this building was also demolished, and the coffin moved again before finally being reburied in catacombs at Warstone Lane Cemetery. So, even after two centuries, John Baskerville has still not got his final wish, although there are occasional attempts to get him buried yet again, this time in un-consecrated ground.

Baskerville left most of his fortune, some £12,000, to his widow Sarah as well as making various bequests to family members and to charity. Sarah carried on with John's printing business for some months after his death, and also maintained the type foundry for another two years. She died in 1788.

Henry Clay, 1738-1812

One man who had probably worked with Baskerville as an assistant was a young man called Henry Clay. In May 1753 he began a six-year apprenticeship with a painter called John Allport, and by 1760 he is thought to have started working for Baskerville. It appears Clay then set up in partnership with another of Baskerville's employees, a japanner called John Gibbons. Together they experimented with different substrate, before Clay came up with the idea of pressing ten thick sheets of unsized rag-paper together, pasted with glue between each sheet. Squeezed between rollers to get rid of any air bubbles, the compressed sheets would then be soaked in linseed oil before being baked in an oven at 1,000 degrees Fahrenheit. The result was a board which had no graining, could be cut and shaped easily, and which had surprising strength, even to the extent of being used for the manufacture of chairs. It also proved to be a superb basis for japanning, since it could be smoothed with pumice stone to give a glass-like finish.

The ability to manufacture boards made out of paper transformed the papier mâché industry. Clay patented the process in 1772, describing it as 'new Improved Paper ware'. The patent refers to 'making, in Paper, High Varnished Pannels or Roofs for Coaches, and all Sorts of Wheel Carriages, and Sedan Chairs, Pannels for Rooms, Doors, and Cabbins of Ships, Cabinets, Bookcases, Screens, Chimney Pieces, Tables, Teatrays, and Waiters.'

The process involved:

pasting several papers upon boards... put in a stove sufficiently hot to deprive them of their flexibility, and at the same time are rubbed over or dipped in oil or varnish, which so immediately drenches into them as to secure them from damps... they are capable of being sawed into different forms, and planed as wood.... then coated with colour and oils sufficient to make the surface even, and then japanned and high varnished.

A dozen years later Clay moved his business to 18 King Street, Covent Garden, and was soon attracting a number of prominent patrons, particularly, the dukes of Bedford and Northumberland, Lord Scarsdale of Kedleston and Horace Walpole of Strawberry Hill. George III was one of his patrons and by 1792 Clay had adopted the title 'Japanner to His Majesty', and had received commissions from both Queen Charlotte and the Prince of Wales.

Clay became associated with what was described as 'Etruscan style'. This became hugely popular in the last two decades of the century, inspired no doubt by the discoveries at Pompeii and Herculaneum, and promoted by the neoclassical designs of the architect Robert Adam. He had designed an entire 'Etruscan Room' for Robert Child at Osterley Park, and Clay's exquisite furniture and effects, decorated to match the surroundings, provided the finishing touch.

Clay's products were frequently decorated with the fashionable chinoiserie style, and he also combined forces with Josiah Wedgwood to produce pieces inlaid with Wedgwood cameos. Clay is especially associated with beautifully decorated tea caddies and painted trays, but the boards were so versatile that they could be used for making panels on the sides of coaches, for the panelled sides to clocks, for snuff boxes and all manner of everyday objects. Clay's success meant that functional objects, often richly decorated, became affordable for large sections of the population. Soon, Clay was employing over 300 men in his factory and he quickly amassed a large fortune.

In 1790 Clay was appointed High Sheriff of Warwickshire, reflecting his prominence as a Midlands industrialist. He revelled in the pomp and ceremony, leading a mounted procession of lawyers in full uniform from his house in the centre of Birmingham. The cavalcade wended its way through the city streets before their Lordships reached the Warwick Assize Court, accompanied by a full complement of church and civic dignitaries and local worthies.

Clay's 'improved paper ware' patent expired in 1802, and after that date a plethora of smaller manufactories popped up in Birmingham, Wolverhampton and indeed throughout the West Midlands. In 1816 Clay's premises were acquired by the firm of Jennens and Bettridge, who continued to make papier mâché until 1864, while opening branches in New York and Paris. By then, the fashion for papier-mâché items was on the wane, but in its heyday Clay and the other papier-mâché manufacturers played a vital part in the expansion of Birmingham as an industrial power base. Matthew Boulton, who started his Soho Manufactory in 1765, may get the headlines for his contribution to Birmingham's rapid rise to become the country's second city, but men such as Baskerville and Clay played their part.

Thomas Boulsover, 1705–1788

On 1 September 1760, the inveterate gossip Horace Walpole wrote a letter to his friend Mr Montagu:

> *As I went to Lord Strafford's I passed through Sheffield, which is one of the foulest towns in England, in the most charming situation, where there are 22,000 inhabitants making knives and scissors. … One man there has discovered the art of plating copper with silver. I bought a pair of candlesticks for two guineas that are quite pretty.*

What Walpole was referring to was the discovery by Thomas Boulsover of a method of fusing copper and silver to produce a material now known as 'Old Sheffield plate'. Even then, eighteen years after the initial discovery of plated silver, the items made from the new material (in this case a pair of candlesticks) were considered 'quite pretty' – a reflection of the fact that design, decoration and form were important, even if the candlesticks were retailing at a fraction of the cost of solid silver items.

Boulsover was born in 1705, and was apprenticed as a cutler in the parish of Ecclesfield (4 miles to the north of Sheffield city centre) to Joseph Fletcher. He qualified in 1726 and married Hannah Dodworth two years later. The pair went on to have ten children, of whom only two reached adulthood. For twenty years Thomas Boulsover was busy making and repairing knives. But if Sheffield's reputation was built on cutlery, it was to receive a huge boost due to the discovery made by Boulsover in 1742/3. There are a number of stories, some no doubt apocryphal, about the curious accident which led to his discovery. One suggests that he was repairing a knife handle, made of silver, holding it in a vice while he applied heat to the silver. Unknown to him, a copper penny was wedged in the vice and, as his concentration wandered, he overheated the silver, causing the silver to fuse with the copper in the penny. However, realistically, this cannot have been the first time that the two metals had been fused. What was new was that Boulsover recognised something very particular about the way the two metals had joined – they were fused in such a way that the 'sandwich' remained in the same proportions, even when beaten or rolled into a lesser thickness.

It was the fact that the copper and silver expanded in unison which was hugely significant. Boulsover started to experiment, noting that the silver melted at a lower temperature than copper. By placing a flat copper sheet under the silver as it was heated and liquified, the silver ran evenly over the copper, then fused with it. It could then be fed through a succession of rollers to make a finer and finer gauge of plated metal, and because copper was a fraction of the cost of silver it meant that the metal was ideal for making items which looked like silver, which could be made into products traditionally made of silver, and which satisfied the growing demand of the public for decorative items which 'wouldn't break the bank'.

To begin with, Boulsover kept the discovery to himself and decided to concentrate on making straightforward items such as buttons. He needed capital to expand the business and approached a friend of the family called Strelley Pegge, and asked for a loan. It was granted, and twelve months later Mr Pegge was surprised to find that Thomas Boulsover wished to pay back not just the interest on the loan, but the entire capital. He apparently explained his success to Mr Pegge by pointing out that whereas he could sell his buttons for a guinea a dozen (21 shillings), the silver in those buttons cost a mere 3 shillings – and the cost of the copper was almost insignificant.

Button-making turned out to be a most profitable exercise and there is a story that,

> when he had been in business some time he sent the sweepings from the workshop floor, which he had taken great care of, to Mr. Read, a silver refiner, in Green Lane, and in a little time they sent him back £100 worth of silver — so much for the value of shop sweepings.

A model of a double-action beam engine from 1840 – a logical development from the work of Newcomen, Watt, Murdoch and Trevithick. See chapters 1 and 3.

When gas lamps were introduced in Pall Mall in January 1807 they caused a sensation – here a sketch by Rowlandson showing public concern about safety issues. See chapter 3.

John Joseph Merlin, inventor, musician – and a whizz-kid on roller skates. See chapter 7.

Rowlandson's *Gouty Gourmands at Dinner* showing two men, one of them in a gouty chair, eating and drinking while being waited on by a host of servants. See chapter 7.

Caricaturists brought home to the British public the full horrors of slavery – here, Gillray's *Barbarities in the West Indies*. See chapters 7 and 8.

Marc Isambard Brunel – see chapter 1.

Gillray's *Anti-saccharrites leaving off sugar* reflecting the boycott of West Indian sugar as part of the anti-slavery campaign. See chapters 7 and 8.

Gillray's *Plumb pudding in Danger* showing Pitt and Napoleon carving up the world. See chapter 7.

Above left and above right: Spode tray from 1800 and Spode creamer from 1805. See chapter 7.

Left: Self portrait of the artist Joseph Wright. See chapter 7.

Below: Joseph Wright's *The Orrery* showing the wonderment of the public when watching scientific instruments in use. See chapter 7.

Above left: Bas-relief portrait of James Stuart by Wedgwood, made from white basalt-ware with green dip. See chapter 7.

Above right: Bust of John Howard over the main entrance of Shrewsbury Prison. See chapter 8.

Above left: Erasmus Darwin, heavyweight doctor, polymath, botanist and inventor. See chapter 3.

Above right: Lord Granville Leveson-Gower by Sir Thomas Lawrence, c.1804. See chapter 7.

Above left: The actress Elizabeth Farren painted by Sir Thomas Lawrence in 1790. See chapter 7.

Above right: Lady Maria Conyngham, wearing a simple Empire-line dress with waist-band, by Sir Thomas Lawrence, 1824. See chapter 7.

A View of Murton Colliery near Seaham, County Durham.

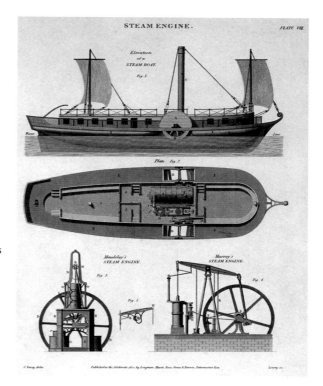

Right: Maudslay developed engines for the early steam-driven paddle steamers. See chapter 2.

Below: Thomas Rowlandson's picture of Astley's Amphitheatre in 1804, showing the ringmaster (probably John Astley) in the centre of the ring, directing a rider standing upright on the back of his horse. See chapter 7.

Above and below: Steam power was a constant source of amusement for caricaturists, who fantasised as to 'where it would all end'. Here, two examples from 1828, just at the dawn of rail travel.

Certainly, Boulsover missed a trick – he never patented the plated-silver process, and therefore missed out on royalties.

Other cutlers in Sheffield could see the opportunities of developing their skills in working with metal, be it in pure silver or by using a cheaper silvery substitute. They diversified away from simply making blades. Craftsmen worked in both metals, silver and plate, and in time Sheffield silversmiths were able to petition parliament for their own Assay Office in 1773. No longer did they have to wait while their products were sent down to London for assaying and return – they could sell direct to the general public, further helping establish the reputation of the city. The fact that the craftsmen could also make buttons, snuff boxes, and decorative fish slices out of a far cheaper metal did nothing to harm this reputation – it just brought the wares to a wider market.

The next development was the introduction in 1770 of a 'double sandwich', i.e. copper plated on both sides with silver. This still left the problem of a copper edge being visible when the metal was cut, but this was overcome, initially by rolling the edge to make a silvered ridge, and subsequently by applying silver wire along the length of the visible copper edge.

It was left to a colleague of Boulsover to develop further commercial possibilities for plated silver. His name was Joseph Hancock, and before long he was manufacturing a wide range of goods, starting with saucepans, then coffee pots, hot-water jugs and moving on to candlesticks. He prospered and emerged as a Master Cutler from 1763 and was one of the thirty 'guardians' appointed to oversee the Sheffield Assay Office.

When Hancock died in 1791, a local newspaper described him, most unfairly, as 'the founder of the plated business in Sheffield, as he was the first person who commenced a manufactory of the goods.' This was to completely overlook Boulsover's involvement in silver plating, which gave a huge boost to the region's economy. In time, more Sheffield plate was made in Birmingham than it was in Sheffield, largely thanks to Matthew Boulton making use of the fused material in his new factory at Soho.

Boulsover seems to have been happy to diversify into other areas where his experience of rolling, rather than hammering, metal could be put to good use. Up until then, wood-cutting saws were hammered from a single piece of steel, and setting the teeth was a difficult and inefficient process. Boulsover developed a system whereby the steel could be fed through rollers and also found a simple way for setting the teeth at an angle. Manpower was soon superseded by horsepower and then by waterpower. To this end, Boulsover opened a mill on the stream below his house at Whiteley Wood, which he had bought from his original benefactor Strelley Pegge in 1757. As a result of his diversification, from 1774 he was being described not as a silver plater in trade directories, but as 'a manufacturer of saws, fenders, edge tools, Casted and Emory, from Sycamore Street'. By the end of the century there were two waterwheels and a steam engine powering the forge's drop hammers at the industrial premises founded by Boulsover in the Porter Valley. It is thought that the forge ceased as a commercial enterprise around 1887.

Boulsover died at his Whiteley Wood home in September 1788 and was buried in St Paul's Church, Sheffield on 12 September. He never made a fortune from his discovery – but others did. The process remained popular until the production of nickel silver, otherwise known as German Silver, in around 1820. This used 60 per cent copper, 20 per cent nickel and 20 per cent zinc – and its nickel content gave it a harder, silvery, appearance which made it more resistant to the copper showing through the top layer due to daily wear and tear. In turn, German silver was largely overtaken by electroplating, which came in during the 1840s. In a way they all proved one thing: there was a commercial appetite for objects which looked like silver, shone and sparkled like silver, but which were in fact made largely from base metals.

There are small memorials to Boulsover in Tudor Square in central Sheffield, and at Wire Mill Dam in the nearby Porter Valley. There is also a small Methodist Chapel still standing, in the grounds of Meadow Farm, adjacent to the site of the old steel-rolling premises. It had been erected by his two surviving daughters and bears the inscription: 'This chapel was built by Mary Mitchell and Sarah Hutton in 1789 in memory of their father Thomas Boulsover, the inventor of Sheffield Plate (1705–1788).' The chapel was later put to use as a cowshed and is now completely disused. Fame has certainly been transient for poor Thomas Boulsover.

Christopher Pinchbeck, c. 1670–1732

Nowadays the term 'pinchbeck' is used in a derogatory sense. It implies something inferior and fake. That is grossly unfair to the man who gave his name to an alloy of copper and zinc which helped transform the jewellery industry in the eighteenth and nineteenth centuries. Back at the start of the Georgian era, jewellery involved silver and gold in an almost pure state – experiments involving electroplating silver with a layer of gold started in 1805. Nine-carat gold was not introduced until 1854 and whereas platinum was identified as a separate metal in the eighteenth century, it was not generally used in the jewellery trade until 1890. White gold followed as recently as 1925.

In the eighteenth century all jewellery was made by hand, and demand for cheaper jewellery came from two different quarters. On the one hand the wealthy were looking for cheaper substitute jewellery which they could take with them when travelling – far less tempting to highway robbers or unscrupulous servants in country inns. On the other hand, increasing numbers of the growing middle class wanted to be able to emulate the fashion for diamond earrings, chokers and fine rings, but without the expense of 'the real thing'.

So, the demand for costume jewellery already existed. Various alloys had been tried, usually linked to brass, but the copies were poor, the alloy usually discoloured and the result was far from convincing. Fancy names such as Tombac, Prince's Metal and Mosaic Gold could not disguise the fact that they were poor imitations of gold. Enter onto the scene one Christopher Pinchbeck – a jeweller, a clockmaker, a showman and a typical Georgian entrepreneur. He was born circa 1670 and lived in the Clerkenwell area of North London. In around 1720 he discovered that whereas brass involved combining one part zinc with three parts copper, an alloy with a much closer resemblance to gold could be obtained by mixing eighty-three parts copper with seventeen parts zinc. Other metals oxidised and discoloured, but this alloy kept its golden lustre for a considerable time, although the coppery colour revealed when holding it up to the light would often betray its guilty (as opposed to gilded) secret.

Pinchbeck did not give his metal a name, but started making beautifully worked pieces of jewellery at affordable prices to sell to the public – but without any attempt to deceive. In July 1721 he placed an advertisement in *Appleby's Weekly Journal* referring to the fact that,

> *Christopher Pinchbeck, inventor and maker of the famous astronomico-musical clocks, is removed from St. George's Court [now Albion Place], to St. John's Lane, to the sign of the 'Astronomico-Musical Clock' in Fleet Street, near the Leg Tavern. He maketh and selleth watches of all sorts, and clocks, as well plain, for the exact indication of time only, as astronomical, for showing the various motions and phenomena of planets and fixed stars.*

In other words, at that stage he saw his automata as the real stars of the show, not the base metal.

However, his trade cards, which can be found in the British Museum and in the V & A museum, describe him as: 'Clock, Watchmaker & Toyman at Pinchbeck's Head in Fleet St and at Tonbridge Wells and the Court of Request – only Maker of the True & Genuine Metal'. His premises on the north side of Fleet Street were situated between Bolt Court and Johnson's Court, and based on the fact that others appeared to try and copy the formula, he was soon enjoying financial success. The 'true and genuine metal' was just what the market was looking for – especially since at about this time a jeweller from Alsace by the name of Georg Friedrich Strass was starting to promote his own brand of rhinestones (originally, rock crystals found along the banks of the River Rhine) as a substitute for diamonds. From this he experimented with making glass with a high lead content, adding to its refractive qualities by adding bismuth and thalium. The artificial gemstones were then mounted on a foil backing, to increase the reflective qualities. Strass opened a factory making artificial gemstones in 1730, and he was awarded the title 'King's Jeweller' in 1734. The artificial gemstones, sometimes called 'strass' but nowadays known as 'paste', were so popular that Strass was able to retire in his early fifties after less than twenty-five years in the business.

Marrying up Strass gemstones with Pinchbeck's 'true and genuine metal' was an obvious development, and once news of Pinchbeck's alloy reached France it featured prominently in the manufacture of watch cases and became known as Pinsbeck, Pincebeck and Pinsbek. In England the name was sometimes abbreviated to 'Pinch'.

Oddly, Christopher Pinchbeck was much more interested in developing his extraordinary musical clocks and automata, although he combined displaying these curiosities with selling his cheap watches, necessaires and so on. In particular he liked to exhibit his wares at Bartholomew Fair, held over a four-day period from 24 August in the Smithfield area of London. The fair drew fun-seekers from all classes of English society, and although it developed a notorious reputation as a venue for thieving and debauchery, it was also a showcase for all manner of attractions. For some reason which is not readily apparent, Pinchbeck chose to team up with a conjuror called Isaac Fawkes. This showman first appeared in advertisements for Southwark Fair in 1722, but it appears that he must have been well known to the public before that date because he was described as having performed before the king, demonstrating his skills with 'Tricks by Dexterity of Hand, with his Cards, Eggs, Corn, Mice, curious India Birds, and Money...'. He would perform his act up to six times a day – and as soon as Bartholomew Fair ended he would move his booth to Southwark Fair, where this advertisement appeared in 1733, announcing that Pinchbeck and Fawkes would:

> Divert the Publick with the following surprising Entertainments at their great
> Theatrical Room at the Queens Arms joining to the Marshalsea Gate. ... The
> diverting and incomparable Dexterity of Hand, perform'd by Mr Pinchbeck who
> causes a Tree to grow out of of a Flower-Pot on the Table, which blossoms and bears
> ripe Fruit in a Minute ... an amazing Musical Clock made by Mr Pinchbeck,
> 2 beautiful moving pictures and performs on several muscial instruments ... a
> curious Machine being the finest Piece of workmanship in the World for moving
> Pictures and other curiosities.

This suggests that Christopher Pinchbeck was actually part of the act, but more generally he simply provided the apparatus used to assist Fawkes in his displays of legerdemain. Pinchbeck placed advertisements in the press, calling his stall the 'Temple of the Muses', 'Grand Theatre of the Muses', or 'Multum in Parvo' (literally, 'a great deal in a small space').

Fawkes had a famous trick of producing an apple tree from seed which 'bore ripe apples in less than a Minute's Time', and in reality relying on a piece of trickery perfected by Pinchbeck. Among Pinchbeck's other works was the 'Venetian Machine', described as being,

> *a fine clock or machine known as the Venetian Lady's Invention, which she employ'd workman to make, that were 17 years contriving; the like of which was never yet made or shown in any other part if the world, for variety of moving pictures, and other curiosities.*

Other works described were,

> *the amazing musical clock, lately made by the famous Mr Pinchbeck, which has two beautiful moving pictures and performs on several instruments, a great variety of fine pieces of Musick, composed by Signior Corelli, Albinoni, Bononcini, Mr Handel and many other celebrated Masters.*

During the fair, from ten in the morning until ten at night, visitors could also see, the following prospects:

> *1. The famous city of Constantinople in Turkey;*
> *2. A fine prospect of the King of Sweden's Pleasure House and garden;*
> *3. The famous city of Venice.*

Fawkes died on 25 May 1732. His widow was stated to have been the recipient of his estate, valued at more than £10,000, and within six months she had married again, this time to Edward, the son of Christopher Pinchbeck. The marriage took place on 17 November – and Christopher, his father, died the very next day, having made his new will one week earlier. Edward then carried on in partnership with the son of Isaac Fawkes, and in particular the pair were instrumental in demonstrating what was presumably Christopher's final invention, known as a 'panopticon'. The handbill promoting the wondrous instrument explained that the panopticon was three sided: one showed a country fair, with musicians and blacksmiths moving in time; the second showed a 'beautiful landskip' (i.e. landscape) with a flowing river and huntsmen; and the third was a shipyard with labourers working on ships to a musical accompaniment. The actual description is rather more elaborate:

First Side
In the first scene is the clock, which besides telling the time shows the high tide times in 30 different sea ports, with the Moon's age, its increase and decrease, full and change, and underneath which is a representation of a Country Fair with a vast variety of Motions too tedious to mention...a Concert of Musick in a tent, of which all the figures have their true actions agreeable to the several airs with which the ear is entertained....

Second side
A great variety of coaches, carts, chaises and horsemen ascending and descending hills and altering their positions, a water mill with the water running from it, swans fighting and feathering themselves, dog and duck hunting, with several other whimsical motions...the upper picture is a smith's shop with men grinding their tools, blowing their bellows, planishing at the anvil, working at the forge etc.

Third side
In the last scene the lower picture represents a ship-carpenters yard with a distant view of the sea. In the yard are workmen corking, carving, sawing in the pit, carrying planks from a pile to the ship....

Note: it plays several pieces of music on various instruments, composed by the best Masters; as Handel, Albononi etc, and imitates an Aviary of birds.

All in all, a cornucopia of splendours for the curious to behold. And that was really what Christopher Pinchbeck was trying to achieve: to amaze, to amuse, to show that things are not always what they seem. He would be horrified to know that his name is synonymous with cheating – his fakery was intended to be something altogether more artistic – and in a way very much in keeping with the Georgian preoccupation with anything new, especially if it was spectacular, combining visual treats with audible musical delights. His alloy was simply a way of demonstrating that man could imitate nature – but it just so happens that in doing so he became 'the father of costume jewellery'.

Others tried to copy his discovery. In 1733 his son Edward placed an advertisement in the *Daily Post*, which warned of cheap imitations. It was headed by the words 'Caution to the Publick':

To prevent for the future the gross imposition that is daily put upon the Publick by a great number of Shop-Keepers, Hawkers, and Pedlars, in and about this town, Notice is hereby given, That the Ingenious Mr. Edward Pinchbeck, at the

'Musical Clock' in Fleet Street, does not dispose of one grain of his curious metal, which so nearly resembles Gold in Colour, Smell and Ductility, to any person whatsoever, nor are the toys made of the said metal, sold by any one person in England except himself: therefore gentlemen are desired to beware of Impostors, who frequent Coffee Houses, and expose for Sale, Toys pretended to be made of this metal, which is a most notorious imposition, upon the Publick.

The advertisement continued with a list of the products then being made out of 'the curious metal':

And Gentlemen and Ladies, may be accommodated by the said Mr. Pinchbeck with the following curious Toys; viz.: Sword-Hilts, Hangers, Cane Heads, Whip Handles for Hunting, Spurs, Equipages [i.e., chatelaines], Watch chains, Tweezers for Men and Women, Snuff-Boxes, Coat Buttons, Shirt Buttons, Knives and forks, Spoons, Salvers, Buckles for Ladies Breasts, Stock Buckles, Shoe Buckles, Knee Buckles, Girdle Buckles, Stock Clasps, Knee Clasps, Necklaces, Corals, and in particular Watches, plain and chased in so curious a manner as not to be distinguished by the nicest eye, from the real gold, and which are highly necessary for Gentlemen and Ladies when they travel, with several other fine pieces of workmanship of all sorts made by the best hands. He also makes Repeating and all other sorts of Clocks and Watches particularly Watches of a new invention, the mechanism of which is so simple, and the proportion so just, that they come nearer the truth than others yet made.

Pinchbeck, father and son, gave the public what it wanted – fine-looking 'must have' products at affordable prices.

French-made watch, made using pinchbeck, circa 1790-1800.

Chapter 5

Working in the Great Outdoors

Above and below: A Dishley ram and ewe, as bred by Robert Bakewell.

Robert Bakewell, 1725–1795

The category of eighteenth-century agricultural innovators is dominated in the public perception by two men: Jethro Tull and 'Turnip' Townshend. Outside of Leicestershire few would name a third contender, Robert Bakewell, and yet he was arguably far more important than either of the other two rivals. Tull and Townshend were both born in 1674, a full half-century before Bakewell. But for all his modern fame, perhaps linked to his memorable name, Tull was a controversial figure, ridiculed and dismissed as something of a crank in his lifetime. Arguably it was only when mechanisation was introduced in the nineteenth century that his invention of the hoe-and-drill came into general use.

Meanwhile Townshend, more correctly Charles Townshend, 2nd Viscount Townshend, was a leading Whig politician who retired from political life to his Norfolk estate where he earned his nickname by extolling the importance of growing turnips as part of a 'Norfolk rotatation'. For this he used four crops: turnips, followed by either barley or oats, then either clover or rye, ending with a crop of wheat. The different crops helped rejuvenate the soil and keep down pathogens and pests in the soil – clover helped put back nitrates, while the deep-rooted turnips drew nutrients which shallower growing plants could not reach.

Having two forage crops, i.e. turnips and clover, in the rotation meant that cattle and sheep could graze the fields throughout the winter – in turn maintaining milk, butter and meat yields and producing manure for the fields all year round. The rotation of crops obviated the need for leaving fields fallow every four or five years – an important factor, since nearly 20 per cent of all arable land was left fallow at any given time in the early 1700s – and meant that farmers could afford to keep livestock in the fields throughout the winter months. Quite rightly, Townshend receives much credit for using his wealth and connections to promote these ideas – but he didn't invent them, borrowing heavily from the farmers of Flanders in modern-day Belgium.

Robert Bakewell has every right to be included alongside these 'greats'. He may not have been the first man to try selective breeding to improve the qualities required by consumers, but his whole approach to improving yields, both from cattle and with sheep, helped make him an inspirational figure.

Robert was born in May 1725, the third in a line of Robert Bakewells who were tenant farmers at Dishley Grange near Loughborough. It was said of his father that he had the reputation of being one 'of the most ingenious and able farmers of his neighbourhood,' according to James Wilson in his book entitled *The evolution of British cattle and the fashioning of breeds.* Wilson states that the father died in 1773, when he was 88 years old, but others generally give his date of death as being 1760.

As a young man, Bakewell was encouraged by his father to tour different parts of the country, and abroad in Holland and Northern Europe, to learn other agricultural methods, to glean new ideas, and to develop an interest – a passion, really – for agricultural reform. He also, most unusually, studied animal anatomy.

All this learning was put into practice when, at the age of around 35, he took over the family farm. To begin with, his improvements were linked to the drainage of the soil in different parts of the farm – some areas were badly drained, and were little more than reed-beds; others dried out so quickly in the free-draining soil that the grass quickly turned dry and whispy. Both extremes were remedied when Bakewell diverted a stream across his fields, draining the one area and irrigating the other. This was done by constructing a canal 1¼ miles long – a not inconsiderable labour of love for a tenant farmer who had to pay for such improvements out of his own pocket. By introducing sluices, sumps and floodgates, he was able to raise and lower the water table to suit the conditions required by the crop being grown. He then faithfully recorded the crop yields based on the irrigation history, and visitors to the farm could see exactly how the grass responded to different conditions.

Various experimental sections were left for inspection – the untreated, the flooded, the fertilised, and so on. One visitor at the time commented that the canal marked 'Mr Bakewell's genius' and particularly mentioned:

> *Mr B's improvements, in this department of rural affairs, are not only extensive, but high; and are rendered the more striking by 'proof pieces' (a good term for experimental patches) left in each site of improvement. Mr Bakewell is in truth a master in the art, and Dishley at present a school in which it might be studied with singular advantage. (Marshall, 1790).*

Not content with such changes, Bakewell deliberately ploughed up the fields which had, since medieval times, been left with a typical ridge-and-furrow surface. The neighbouring Doubting Thomas's apparently felt that he was 'burying good land to bring up bad' and threatened to sue him because they thought that his new-fangled water meadows would cause floodwater to escape onto their land. Eventually Bakewell countered by constructing banks around the flooded areas so that the water was contained within his boundaries.

In 1770 his farm was visited by Arthur Young, the English writer on agricultural matters who was later to become Secretary to the Board of Agriculture. His opinion was that the grass yield was ten-times higher in the areas treated by Bakewell, compared with the yields achieved by other farmers nearby. In particular, Bakewell was able to take four crops of grass in a single calendar year. Young also noted that at that time Bakewell was farming 440 acres, a quarter of it arable. The rest was kept for grass, and on the land he was able to keep 60 horses, 400 large sheep and over 150 cattle of various breeds and assorted sizes. In practice Bakewell was able to over-winter 170 cattle on his land, giving him the opportunity to assess and develop the qualities of different breeds from one season to the next, rather than killing them and having the meat salted down each winter.

On one occasion Arthur Young was to write: 'Small properties, much divided, prove the greatest source of misery that can possibly be conceived, and has operated to such a degree and extent in France, that a law ought certainly to be made to render all division below a certain number of arpens illegal.' (An arpen was a French unit of land measurement, equivalent to roughly 0.85 of an acre). But Young approved of the farming methods of Bakewell, and would have seen that he divided up his land into 10-acre fields, marked by hawthorn hedges, but also that he kept several small grassed areas (less than one acre) close to the farmhouse where he could keep sheep and cattle isolated and under close supervision. Young must have been impressed that Bakewell could continue to feed such a large number of animals throughout the winter. Root vegetables such as carrots, turnips and potatoes were grown for winter feeding, as well as vetches, varieties of kale and cabbage.

But Bakewell's success, and his great fame at the time, rested with his experiments in animal selection – with sheep, with cattle, and to a limited extent with horses. These experiments have to be seen in context of the huge population explosion which occurred in the Georgian period. A population in England of roughly 5 million in 1700, largely living in rural areas, had mushroomed to perhaps 10 million by 1800, many of them living in towns and conurbations such as Manchester, Birmingham and Liverpool. London in the same period grew from perhaps 600,000 to well over a million people. All those extra mouths needed feeding, and that is why the Bakewell experiments in selective breeding are so important. Up until the middle of the seventeenth century, sheep were primarily bred for their wool, and cattle were mainly bred for milk or as beasts of burden (e.g oxen).

The other thing to remember is that eighteenth-century tastes were very different to our own. Our palettes have adapted to eating beef with virtually no fat attached, and we scorn fatty mutton in favour of leaner cuts of meat, whereas back in 1700, what the great majority of the working population wanted was a nice piece of fatty meat which could be boiled for an age with vegetables, barley and so on to give a warming, tasty and, above all, filling meal. William Marshall, writing in the *Rural Economy of the Midland Counties*, posed the question in 1790:

> *To what stomach can mutton like this be grateful? The answer held out is 'fat mutton is the poor man's mutton; it goes farther than lean; and has of course, a smaller proportion of bone than lean mutton. A poor man gives eightpence a pound for bacon, but only five pence for fat mutton.'*

Marshall continues:

> *This semblance between fat mutton and bacon is not altogether imaginary. When salted, and kept some time in pickle, even the palette perceives a strong resemblance.*

He concluded that if the farmers of Leicestershire:

> *can really supply the markets with good bacon ... grown on sheep's bones instead of producing it as heretofore upon those of swine ... at fourpence or fivepence a pound, their country will certainly have some reason to thank them.*

Bakewell started by touring the country looking for what he considered the ideal animals to start with – and analysed the qualities he was looking for. Typically, sheep at the time were big-boned, whereas Bakewell was looking for an animal with a low bone to bodyweight ratio, one which would fatten quickly and produce the maximum amount of saleable meat in the shortest possible time. Given that previously sheep had been used for their wool, not for their carcass, this was a total turnaround. Having chosen the examples he wished to develop, Bakewell then deliberately bred to fix the characteristics he wanted – especially by breeding father with daughter, mother with son, or brother with sister, in a process known as 'breeding-in-and-in'. Bakewell was not the first to use this form of selective breeding and the expression 'breeding-in-and-in' was almost certainly originated by the horse breeders of Newmarket.

Soon, Bakewell established a flock of sheep unlike anything previously seen, known as the Dishley or 'New Leicester'. The 'Old Leicester' was considered a somewhat ugly-looking animal with a large frame, heavy bones, long legs and angular features, making it look somewhat like a goat. The 'New Leicester' was barrel-shaped, short legged and, for maximum results, could be killed at two years of age (as against three or four years with the traditional variety). William Marshall concluded that the new breed of improved sheep was of more value to the consumer, 'for while mankind eats flesh, he throws away the bone'.

Furthermore, the meat on the New Leicester was described as being fine-grained and with a superior flavour. In comparison, the meat of the Old Leicester was sponge-like and coarse. Above all, the new breed was a sheep with a large amount of fat on what was termed the foreflank – the area immediately behind the shoulder. Nowadays we would be horrified at such fatty meat, but to the working masses of the eighteenth Century, it was manna from heaven!

Bakewell introduced a number of interesting measures to aid his breeding programme. He generally kept a control animal – not one which had been bred by him – and exposed it to the exact same conditions as his chosen sheep, so that he could demonstrate that any difference in weight, size and so on was down to breeding and not to the amount of feed etc. He also made sure that the ram chosen for breeding purposes was kept 'ready for action' by using a 'teaser ram' to find out when a particular ewe was in season. This inferior ram would not be allowed to mate, but with an 'apron' or nappy tied around its girth preventing it from achieving penetration, it would run with the flock and try and mount any ewe coming in to season. This showed Bakewell exactly when each ewe was receptive. That ewe would then be brought into a separate enclosure where the stock ram would be introduced – a method which meant that a ram might serve up to 140 ewes in a season. The stock ram wasted none of its energies in chasing unreceptive ewes, and Bakewell was able to charge somewhere between 50 and 300 guineas per ram, per season. The *Leicester Journal* even carried a report of 'a fact almost incredible', that one particular ram earned Bakewell a staggering 1,200 guineas in hiring fees in a single season.

However, Bakewell was not one to let the results of his breeding programmes out of his sight – he would spend the summer months crossing hundreds and hundreds of miles of country roads, calling on farms to see how the offspring were developing, taking notes and generally keeping tabs on them – to the extent of being accused of spying by some of his less appreciative brethren.

In particular Bakewell developed the idea of letting out his stud rams for the mating season (around four months) and William Marshall gives an interesting picture about how the transport arrangements worked:

The usual time of beginning to send out is the middle of September. The means of conveyance, carriages of two wheels, with springs, or hung in slings; some of them being large enough to hold four rams. In these they travel from 20 to 30 miles a day, being sent in this way sometimes two or three hundred miles.

Having agreed a hiring fee, the hirer did not have to pay one penny until the end of the season, and then only if the ram had performed on an agreed number of occasions. If the ram died, the entire risk was on Mr Bakewell – the hirer paid nothing.

One other highly important introduction made by Bakewell was the formation of the Dishley Society in 1783. It was to be the forerunner of all subsequent breed associations formed to protect the purity of stock. Bakewell was to be its president until 1795, the year of his death. It was, in effect, a cartel – and a very effective one at that. Its aim was to preserve the purity of the Dishley breed, and to promote the interests of the breeders. There were thirteen separate rules to which all members had to adhere – from only hiring out rams belonging to members, to imposing a 10-guinea minimum hiring charge. It was intended to create a monopoly, which generated very considerable profits for its members.

However, Bakewell was not particularly motivated by money – his obsession with breeding 'the perfect animal' was far more important. He was also renowned for his efforts at animal welfare – his sheep and cattle were described as being particularly docile and healthy, and the Bakewell home became a mecca for visitors from around the country, and from France, keen to see the results which Bakewell was achieving. For these visitors Bakewell proved to be extremely generous with his time and hospitality. He showed his visitors the grassland and allowed them to inspect the livestock, exhibited one at a time for their inspection. Bakewell also displayed the examples of pickled carcasses, demonstrating the weight gains but actually giving very little away as to how he achieved such spectacular results.

Bakewell was a pioneer in breeding cattle for beef. He chose the long-horned heifer and crossed it with a Westmoreland bull, and eventually produced a massive animal weighing twice as much as the national average. He also used selective breeding to produce an improved black cart-horse – later leading to the Shire horse. These proved useful to the army, and were used on Bakewell's farm for draft purposes (in place of oxen).

Bakewell was convinced of the need to charge premium prices for hiring out his prize animals – not, it would seem, in order to maximise profits for himself, but because he believed that only by charging a high price would the farmer having the use of a hired bull bother to select the best cows for mating. In his mind, high prices ensured that the best qualities of the breed would be maintained, a decision which led John Monk, in his *General View of the Agriculture of the County of Leicester,* published in 1794, to remark:

I myself saw a heifer sold at Mr Pierce's sale, near Northampton, for eighty guineas; and a few days after, as she was driven through Leicester, a party of farmers standing together valued her at about eight pounds. I was likewise informed that Mr Bakewell had let a bull to a gentleman for fifty guineas for the season. The gentleman dying in the interim, and the executors not knowing anything of this transaction, sold the bull at auction with the rest of the cattle. When the season was over, Mr Bakewell sent for his bull, and, after investigating the matter, found, to his great surprize, that the bull had been sold to a butcher for about eight pounds, who had killed it, and sold it for 2½d per pound.

Monk went on to explain that the executors declined to pay, saying that as the bull was sold at an auction attended by a great number of knowledgeable farmers, it could be taken that £8 was a fair price. Bakewell sued on the contract, and as Monk says,

people appearing as witnesses on the trial who were acquainted with their breed, and making oath that Mr Bakewell had not over-valued his bull, a verdict was given in favour of Mr Bakewell to the full amount, with costs of suit.

Despite the extraordinary figures charged for hiring rams and bulls, Bakewell was not good at managing his finances and got into financial difficulties. He was declared bankrupt – and only the generosity of his fellow farmers (members of the Dishley Society) baled him out. Bakewell died on 1 October 1795; he was unmarried and for some years his nephew carried on the family farm. However, within a very short space of time the breeds which Bakewell had developed all went out of favour, to be replaced by others. Tastes changed – the public demanded leaner meat, and thanks to the efforts of one of Bakewell's protégés by the name of Charles Colling, cattle with short horns almost eradicated the long-horn variety. The Durham short-horn proved to be just as cost-effective to rear, pound for pound, and gave a higher milk yield. Equally, the sheep we know and recognise today soon replaced the Dishley or New Leicester. But that is not to say that Bakewell was wrong – indeed his lasting legacy is the fact that those changes which took place after his lifetime all occurred because farmers followed his methods.

James Wilson, mentioned earlier, commented on Bakewell's selection methods with the following words:

(a) he was an unparalleled judge of stock;
(b) he was at enormous pains to secure the best stock in the country for that purpose;
(c) having secured these, he bred from remarkably close relations; and
(d) he ruthlessly eliminated undesirable stock.

Bakewell achieved great renown in his lifetime, not least because of his willingness to prove his researches by producing evidence – in the form of test areas of land, comparisons, charts and display items. Even the reigning monarch (George III, often referred to as 'Farmer George') commissioned a royal inquiry as to his 'new discovery in stock breeding'.

Some of his initiatives merely put into practice what others had tried before – for instance, his work in creating water meadows echoes the work done fifty years before down on the Somerset levels. There, Dutch water engineers who had been brought to Britain when the Dutch William of Orange became king, showed what could be achieved by proper drainage and irrigation. He was not by any means the first to experiment with selective breeding – it had been used for many years in the horse-racing industry, ending up with the breeding of the unbeaten horse Eclipse in 1764, whose DNA is found today in 95 per cent of all modern racehorses. But his scientific approach demonstrated the very significant changes which could be made, over a comparatively short period of time, compared with natural selection. Even Darwin recognised this in his *On the Origin of Species*, describing Bakewell's methods of 'artificial selection' (as opposed to natural selection) and noting how differences occurred, even with domesticated animals, where they were reared in different environments. When Darwin wrote *The Variation of Animals and Plants under Domestication* in 1868 he explained that his first interest in evolution, as well as his later thinking on the subject, was inspired by the work of farmers such as Robert Bakewell.

Bakewell played an important, almost inspirational, part in the Agricultural Revolution which enabled England to feed its burgeoning population, but no one has thought to name a rock band after him (as with Jethro Tull). Fame is indeed a strange bedfellow…

Humphry Repton, 1752–1818

The general public are happy to have one gardening colossus from the eighteenth century: Capability Brown. He was certainly a man of huge influence in garden design, affecting our taste in rolling countryside, distant vistas and 'natural' ponds and rivers, but he was by no means the only landscape gardener worthy of note, yet his very fame seems to detract from the reputations of everyone else. When the tercentenary of Brown's birth was marked in 2016, it garnered far more attention than the 2018 celebration marking the two centuries since the death of another remarkable man, Humphry (no 'e') Repton. Brown got commemorative postage stamps, Repton did not.

Repton succeeded Brown in the sense that Repton took up where Brown left off. By the date of Brown's death in 1783, Repton was already 31 and had a chain of business failures behind him – you name it, he had tried it, and in each case the result was the same: financial disaster. However, once he turned to full-time landscape gardening at the age of 36, he didn't look back.

He was never just another Capability Brown clone. Brown was personally involved in the creation of a number of hugely influential gardens, although often this meant destroying an equal number of existing important and well-loved formal gardens. Some have nicknamed him 'the destroyer', tearing up parterres and formal borders throughout the country. Certainly, the three greatest baroque gardens in the land, at Chatsworth, Blenheim and Petworth, were all destroyed between 1757 and 1760, to make way for flocks of sheep chewing contentedly across rolling grassland. As the poet R.O. Cambridge remarked, 'he hoped to die before Brown so that he could see heaven before it was 'improved'. The architect William Chambers was also no lover of Brown's work, dismissing the garden designs with the words 'they differ very little from common fields, so closely is vulgar nature copied in most of them'.

Repton, on the other hand, generally tweaked and made minor amendments – no one could accuse him of outright vandalism. Creating a surprise vista around a corner or bringing a driveway up to the main house via a serpentine curve (instead of a full-frontal straight approach) was Repton's hallmark. Brown liked ha-has – hidden ditches enabling sheep to graze as if right up to the house lawn; Repton stuck up a decorative fence on top of the bank, so that it emphasised the control he had over the environment. He also had a number of commissions to develop parks and squares in London, bringing green into the heart of the metropolis. So, we have Repton to thank for the design of the central gardens at the heart of the development of Bloomsbury. Originally, Repton gave us the greenery of Russell Square, Bedford Square, Tavistock Square and Fitzroy Square. The planners, and wartime bombing, have greatly reduced their significance and splendour, although Russell Square remains as an impressive and large piece of 'country in the city'. Repton himself described his overall plan, saying:

> a few years hence… this square may serve to record, that the Art of Landscape Gardening in the beginning of the nineteenth century was not directed by whim or caprice, but founded on a due consideration of utility as well as beauty, without a bigoted adherence to forms and lines, whether straight, or crooked, or serpentine.

One other important difference between the two men was that Brown did a design-and-build service. He undertook the commissions from start to finish, overseeing every detail. Repton preferred to submit design ideas, leaving it to the individual owner to decide how and when to implement them, either in whole or in part.

Another area where Brown and Repton differed was in the transitional area between house and garden: Brown brought the rolling parkland right up to the sides of the house; Repton brought in terraced walkways, overhanging arbours for elegant walks around the building – even formal flower beds so that fragrances and colours could be appreciated close-to by house guests. In doing so he softened many of Brown's original designs, making them much closer to modern tastes.

One other fundamental difference between the two men was that Brown was almost secretive about his methods. He was a brilliant water engineer, and many of his drainage schemes were buried underground, out of view. He didn't see the need to publish books giving away his secrets, preferring to be paid there and then by the householder rather than reach down to what were perhaps more middle-class, aspirational, garden owners. Repton provided such people with 'an ideas book' so that they could make their own country estates, albeit on a much smaller scale than Brown's masterpieces.

Above all, Repton was a marketeer: he knew how to sell his schemes. Not only did he hand out his business cards, conveniently printed with a picture of himself surveying the garden and lakeland setting of an imagined work in progress, but he came up with a brilliant marketing tool – his little red book. It is estimated that there were over 400 of these, each bound in a red morocco leather cover. Each started off with a description of the estate – where it was situated, its acreage, its division between woodland and farm, the approach and elevation of the main residence and so on.

Each book would then go on to show how improvements could be made – perhaps a glimpse through the trees of a distant church spire, a half-view of a grand house, or a section of winding river. Repton would demonstrate these subtle changes with a hand-painted view which would nowadays be replaced by computer graphics. Lifting a corner of the picture revealed a flap, and lifting the flap showed how the vista could be changed. 'Before' and 'After' views were a sensational tool for demonstrating what could be achieved, and if a picture told a thousand words, these alternative pictures did so a thousand times more effectively. Some of the books were commissioned by estate owners who never intended to implement the changes, but they kept the little red book because it so beautifully illustrated the potential of their estates. Today many of them are available online, or have been reprinted as facsimile copies. They are stunning, tidying away unsightly quarry edges, revealing lakes and river views, and giving proportion and balance to distant vistas.

There was little in his background and early life to suggest a horticultural calling. Repton had been born in 1752 in Bury St Edmunds. His father was a collector of Excise Duties, and later on developed a transport business. Humphry was sent to the local grammar school until he was 12, and at that point was sent to Holland with a view to learning Dutch and preparing to be a merchant. He ended up staying with an extremely wealthy merchant and returned to Norwich at 16, having acquired a fondness for the opportunities which money could buy. He signed up as an apprentice to a local textile merchant, before getting married to a local girl called Mary Clarke in 1773. His own textile business folded, and when his parents both died in 1778 he used his modest inheritance to buy a small estate at Sustead, some

20 miles north of Norwich. From here he tried numerous ventures – as a farmer, as a journalist, as a playwright, as an artist and as a political agent. All were met with failure. When his neighbour William Windham was appointed Lord Lieutenant of Ireland in 1783, he accompanied him to Ireland in his capacity as private secretary. Windham's appointment only lasted a month and Repton ended up significantly out of pocket, especially after taking his travel expenses into account.

In keeping with his image as a gentleman antiquarian, he returned after sketching scenes in Dublin, North Wales and in Bath, before embarking on a venture which exhausted almost all his capital. He met up with a Bath businessman called John Palmer, who had a grandiose idea for reforming the system whereby mail coaches operated out of London through to major cities such as Bath. Given that his father had owned and run a business hauling wagons and operating stagecoaches, young Repton thought that this was a good investment. And so it was – for Palmer, who gained government support, and ultimately achieved considerable fame and fortune. But for Repton, he gained nothing from the venture and returned to Norfolk with a much-depleted bank balance. This led him to move home in 1788, with his wife and four young children in tow, to a small house near Romford in Essex. It was there that he decided to combine his interest in botany with his love of sketching, in a belief that he could make improvements to the landscape by viewing it from the perspective of an artist. He came up with the phrase 'landscape gardener', and to him, gardening was an art form, using trees, plants, lakes and pathways to create his ideal picture. His local contacts proved invaluable, and soon he was enjoying financial success. No matter that he had no previous experience or training – he had a good eye, the gift of the gab, and the ability to convey ideas to impressionable clients.

In 1793 Repton published the first of his three major books on garden design: *Sketches and Hints on Landscape Gardening*. It was to be followed in 1803 with *Observations on the Theory and Practice of Landscape Gardening* and by *Fragments on the Theory and Practice of Landscape Gardening* in 1816. Much of what he wrote drew on the material he had already assembled in his Red Books, but the works meant that landowners, both in this country and in America, could see 'the tricks of the trade', and decide how to make improvements. His 1803 work *Observations* set out the four basic tenets of Repton's design work:

The perfection of landscape gardening consists in the four following requisites. First, it must display the natural beauties and hide the defects of every situation. Secondly, it should give the appearance of extent and freedom by carefully disguising or hiding the boundary. Thirdly, it must studiously conceal every interference of art. However expensive by which the natural scenery is improved; making the whole appear the production of nature only; and fourthly, all objects of mere convenience or comfort, if incapable of being made ornamental, or of becoming proper parts of the general scenery, must be removed or concealed.

Many of Repton's commissions were for fairly small projects, although he is associated with garden designs at Betchworth House in Surrey as well as at Dyrham Park near Bath, Longleat in Wiltshire, Tatton Park in Cheshire, and Woburn Abbey. At Woburn he introduced the idea of themed gardens – a Japanese Garden, an American Garden, and a separate arboretum; Woburn remains as perhaps the most intact Repton landscape which the public can get to see. Another Repton marvel, at Endsleigh in Devon, is now a hotel.

During the 1790s Repton developed a working arrangement with the aspiring young architect John Nash. The idea was that Nash would design the house, Repton the garden. Nash got to be associated with Repton's name and reputation as the designer of the moment, and two of Repton's sons were given jobs in Nash's design studio. It should have worked, but it didn't, and in 1800 Nash dissolved the partnership amid much acrimony and without paying Repton the commission which was his due.

The bitterness between Nash and Repton then got tied up with the plan by the Prince of Wales to build his Brighton pavilion. Repton and his sons spent much time interpreting and adapting the Indian-inspired drawings in the 1805 publication of William Daniell's *Oriental Scenery*. Repton even got as far as producing a fine Red Book to showcase his designs for an Indian–Saracenic pleasure dome. Nash rubbished the idea, yet when Repton lost the contest to design the pavilion Nash promptly submitted his own designs, very similar to Repton's. It was Nash who got the contract.

The high-point of Repton's career had already passed, and commissions declined in the aftermath of the Napoleonic Wars. Inflation and the dreaded Income Tax had taken its toll on wealthy families, to the extent that money to spend on landscaping gardens was scarce. To make matters worse, Repton's carriage overturned on an icy road in January 1811, causing him spinal damage. He also suffered from an acute heart condition and was left in constant pain, generally confined to a wheelchair, and this made site inspections extremely difficult.

Repton died on 24 March 1818 at his home in Hare Street, probably as a result of a heart attack. He was buried in accordance with his detailed instructions, at Aylsham church, where a fine memorial can still be seen.

What then of his legacy? Certainly, Brown was the main architect of naturalism, but somehow his influence was on the big estates – the wealthy landowners. What Repton did was bring these ideas within reach of less wealthy patrons. You did not have to own your own quaint church or distant pleasing building – but you could 'borrow' a view of it through your trees. His plans could be adapted to quite modest gardens, and for that he has arguably had a more lasting impact on British gardens than his illustrious and oh-so-capable predecessor.

The trade card of Humphry Repton.

Chapter 6

Scientific Endeavours

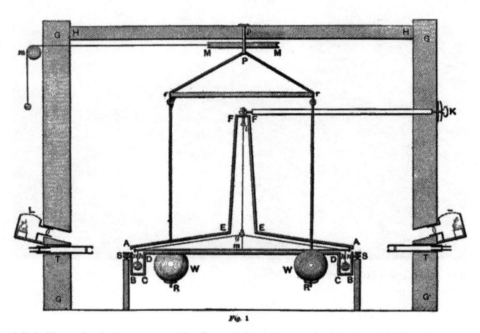

Michell's torsion balance, as used by Cavendish to measure the density of the Earth.

John Michell, 1724–1793

One of the reasons some men may have escaped public acclamation was that they were so far ahead of their time that during their lifetime, nobody appreciated their greatness: one such man was John Michell.

He left no portrait, he left no fortune, no medals, no volumes of notes. He was a rector in the Yorkshire village of Thornhill, where his wife was a local shepherd tending a small flock of sheep. He was also a brilliant astronomer, excelled in mathematics, was a geologist of note, experimented with magnetism, and wrote papers on gravitation. He was the first to postulate the existence of black holes; he explained the way that double stars were attracted to each other, and came up with ideas which were totally overlooked for a century-and-a-half before being 'reinvented'. He devised a way of establishing the mass of the earth and, at a time when earthquakes were thought to have been caused by divine displeasure and consisted of winds rushing through subterranean tunnels, came up with a scientific theory to show how earthquakes generated seismic waves. He also published a treatise on artificial magnets. Small wonder that the epithet 'Father of ...' has been applied to him, both for seismology and magnetometry.

Michell was born in 1724 in Eakring in Nottinghamshire, and was admitted to Queens' College Cambridge at the age of 18. A succession of academic qualifications followed before he was appointed to various posts at the College, successively teaching Hebrew, Arithmetic, Geometry and Greek. He was made a member of the Royal Society in 1760. In 1762 he was appointed Woodwardian professor of geology at Cambridge – up until that time known as the Professorship of Fossils.

In 1764 the 39-year-old Mitchell, described as being 'a little short Man, of a black Complexion, and fat', married Sarah Williamson, who was said to be a 'young lady of considerable fortune', but she died within the year. Being married was a bar to him continuing as an academic in college and he had therefore taken up an appointment as rector at Thornhill, a position which he was to hold for twenty-six years. In 1773 he married Anne Brecknock and together they had a daughter, Mary. Both wife and daughter survived Michell when he died on 21 April 1793; he was buried in the churchyard of St Michael's Church at Thornhill. By his Will he left his scientific equipment to Queens' College.

In 1750 Michell had published his *Treatise on Artificial Magnets*, putting forward the theory that the forces of attraction and repulsion between the poles of different magnets were governed by an inverse square. If, for example, the distance between magnets were to be doubled, the force between them would decrease by a factor of four. He also devised a cheap way of making magnetic needles – up until then these had to be made out of magnetite, a naturally formed mineral containing iron oxide. Michell found that it was far simpler to take a strip of steel and rub it against a piece of magnetite. The steel became permanently magnetised, and held an attraction even stronger than the original magnet. It was a discovery which was to be important both in maritime navigation and in mining.

His work on earthquakes and seismology had been developed in the aftermath of the 1755 Lisbon earthquake, which had resulted in the total destruction of large parts of the city. On 1 November of that year, a quake occurred which is believed to have killed up to 100,000 people; either from the collapse of buildings or in the firestorm that followed, or from drowning in the tsunami which came afterwards. Michell's paper, entitled *Conjectures concerning the Cause and Observations upon the Phaenomena of Earthquakes*, propounded the idea of faults in the underlying layers making up the earth's crust, and suggested that the force spread like waves through the ground, ultimately causing the tsunami which so catastrophically swamped the devastated city. In his words, an earthquake involved 'shifting masses of rock miles below the surface', and he suggested that a large quake was always followed by aftershocks. The shockwaves were explained by Michell in his paper with the words:

> *For the proof of ... the wave-like motion of the earth, we may appeal to many accounts of earthquakes: a gentleman in Jamaica (1687) saw the ground rise like the sea in a wave, as the earthquake passed along.... In New England (1755) ... a gentleman says the earth rose in a wave.... In Lisbon (1755) the wave-like motion was propagated to far greater distances... through all of Germany, in Denmark, Sweden, Norway, and the British Isles.*

He was also able to estimate the epicentre of the quake, and to calculate its magnitude.

Slightly less easy to explain, Michell came up with the concept of 'dark stars' – what we now term as 'black holes'. He suggested that in the universe there might exist massive stars with such a huge gravitational pull that this could cause an escape velocity higher than the speed of light. These dark stars could be detected by examining the effect of that gravitational pull upon other stars.

In 1767 he published a paper on star groupings, suggesting that these were not random. He took as his example the Pleiades star cluster, and using his probability theory calculated that the likelihood of such a grouping being produced by chance was roughly one in half-a-million. In his own words:

> *...from the apparent situation of the stars in the heavens, there is the highest probability, that, either by the original act of the Creator, or in consequence of some general law (such perhaps as gravity) they are collected together in great numbers in some parts of space, whilst in others there are either few or none.*

Up until that point in time, astronomers had noted 'double stars'. Michell's probability theory suggested that these double stars were not in the same part of the sky by mere chance – they were bound together by the forces of gravity, revolving around each other. William Herschel and his diminutive sister Caroline spent years cataloguing such binary stars, finally proving that Michell's probability theory was correct. Herschel was a fan of Michell, and following the latter's death he purchased Michell's 10ft-long telescope with a 30in reflective mirror for the price of £30. It is worth remembering that Herschel was a most accomplished maker of telescopes, and his purchase is a testament to what a superb instrument Michell had been using.

Michell's final contribution to science was saved until after his death. He had developed a torsion balance, intended to weigh the earth. The torsion balance involved measuring the gravitational effect of different masses – in this case the earth as opposed to two lead weights – on a couple of lead spheres hung on ropes. Michell died before the experiment could be carried out and it was left to his friend Henry Cavendish to assemble the balance, make the calculations, and come up with a figure for the earth's mass which is within one per cent of what modern scientists calculate it to be.

Here was a man who nowadays would be a certainty for a Nobel Prize – or in the eighteenth century you would have expected at the very least the Copley Medal and a pension from the state. So how come the American Physical Society has described Michell as being 'so far ahead of his scientific contemporaries that his ideas languished in obscurity, until they were reinvented more than a century later'? The answer was provided by the same Society when they stated that while 'he was one of the most brilliant and original scientists of his time, Michell remains virtually unknown today, in part because he did little to develop and promote his own path-breaking ideas.'

In the end, the rector who abandoned his career in academia because he got married was just too modest and too unfashionable to be understood by his contemporaries. It was not until the 1970s that his published papers were re-examined and the significance of his ideas about 'dark stars' was fully appreciated.

John Dalton, 1766–1844

On 26 July 1844 a frail 77-year-old man recorded the last of some 200,000 meteorological observations. He had suffered a number of strokes in recent years, and that night he fell from his bed and was found dead the following day by his attendant. Death marked the end of a remarkable man – remarkable enough for him to be accorded a civic funeral in his adopted city of Manchester. Some 40,000 mourners filed past his coffin as he lay in state at Manchester Town Hall, and when he was buried in the city's Ardwick Cemetery on 12 August, his funeral procession was over a mile long. The cortege included over 100 carriages and transported all the great and the good of the city to the cemetery, along with representatives of the scientific community from far and wide.

The deceased was John Dalton – a man so modest and unassuming in his lifetime that he would have been horrified at all the fuss. He was an old-fashioned Quaker – a man who not only dressed in the severe puritanical garb of Quakers, but whose speech marked him out as a Quaker, and whose life was firmly based in Quaker traditions. Never banging his own drum, shunning personal possessions and anything showy or ostentatious, here was a man who, if he had been born two centuries later, would no doubt have been lauded with honours, awarded a knighthood and praised for his contribution to all branches of science.

Back in the Georgian era, 'science' covered all fields of human knowledge, whereas we tend to think of separate branches of science, such as physics, biology, chemistry and so on. But such artificial categories meant nothing to John Dalton – his discoveries crossed the boundaries and although he was one of the founders of the science of meteorology he was also renowned as a chemist and as an atomic theorist.

It all seemed so unlikely when he was born into a poor Quaker household near Cockermouth in Cumberland in September 1766. His father, Joseph, was a weaver, his grandfather, Jonathan, a cobbler. His mother, Deborah, bore six children but only three survived to adulthood, John being the youngest. He had a limited schooling at a local Quaker school run by John Fletcher and, when Fletcher retired, the running of the school was taken over by John Dalton's elder brother Jonathan. From the age of 12, John was helping his brother with the teaching, while continuing his own education in his spare time.

At this tender age he was also earning a little money while in service with a wealthy Quaker family in the area, headed by a man called Elihu Robinson – someone who was a knowledgeable observer of weather patterns and who kindled the young boy's interest in the new science of meteorology. This eventually resulted in Dalton starting his own diary of weather observations when he was 21. It was a diary which he kept for the next fifty-seven years, with tens of thousands of detailed records and comments.

As a teenager he had moved with his brother Jonathan to help run a Quaker school belonging to George Bewlay at Kendal, some 45 miles away from his home village. The school taught around sixty children. By the time he was 19 he had been made principal of the school, a position he held until he was 26. During that time he developed an interest in mathematics, being encouraged in his studies by John Gough, who, although completely blind, was an accomplished natural and experimental philosopher. Dalton was able to assist Gough both by reading articles to him and by writing up his notes, as well as preparing diagrams and calculations. In exchange Dalton was helped by Gough in his Latin and Greek studies. Dalton later referred to Gough as a 'prodigy in scientific attainments', and dedicated his first two books to his friend and mentor.

In 1793, at the age of 27, Dalton published his first book, entitled *Meteorological Observations and Essays*. No one took much notice of it, even though it contained a number of original ideas which were subsequently developed by Dalton and formed the basis of later works. Also in 1793, Dalton was appointed teacher of mathematics and natural philosophy at the dissenting academy known as New College in Manchester. This gave him a salary of £80 a year, and the position probably owed much to a bit of lobbying on his behalf carried out by John Gough. He remained there for seven years before the college's lack of financial security forced Dalton to leave and to earn a living giving private lessons. From then on he gave coaching in mathematics and scientific subjects for 2 shillings an hour, but with the advantage that he had the freedom to manage his time so that he could pursue his experiments and work on his various theories.

On 3 October 1794, while working at New College, he was elected a member of the Manchester Literary and Philosophical Society, giving him access to a laboratory for the first time. He soon contributed his first paper to the Society, on *Extraordinary facts relating to the vision of colours*, which was the first ever publication on colour blindness. This was a condition which both John and his brother Jonathan suffered from, and which John recognised as being a hereditary condition. Colour blindness is still sometimes referred to as 'Daltonism'. John Dalton put forward the hypothesis that his condition was caused by discoloration of the liquid medium of the eyeball. Dalton bequeathed his eyes to be preserved after his death and studied to see what could be learnt from them about colour blindness. More recent tests show that in fact he suffered from a different and less-common form of colour blindness – one in which he could only perceive blue, purple and yellow. Other colours – red, orange and green – all appeared as a different shade of yellow, a condition now known as deuteranopia.

Dalton continued to be intrigued by climate and weather condition. He held the belief, unpopular at the time, that the atmosphere was made up of 80 per cent nitrogen and 20 per cent oxygen. He started to give consideration to questions about how mixed gases were made up; how steam reacted to being placed in a vacuum; the properties of gases undergoing thermal expansion and the theory of evaporation. These four topics formed a series of lectures delivered to the Manchester Literary and Philosophical Society during the month of October 1801, and were published as essays in the Memoirs of the Society in 1802.

In the following year he published an important paper outlining his famous law of partial pressures. His studies helped establish meteorology on a firm footing to the extent that another scientist, John Frederic Daniell, went on to describe John Dalton as the 'father of meteorology'. During the period between 1817 and his death in 1844 he went on to contribute some 117 papers published as *Memoirs of the Literary and Philosophical Society of Manchester* on topics as diverse as the colour of the sky, how rain and dew are formed, and on how spring water originates. He showed calculations on measuring the volume of water in rivers, and examined the thermal and physical properties of gases and vapours.

Dalton was beginning to enjoy a considerable reputation as a scientist, both in Britain and in Europe (particularly in France). In 1803 he was invited by the Royal Society in London to deliver a series of lectures. A repeat invitation followed in 1809 and in the following year he was invited to become a fellow of the Royal Society.

It was a position he declined, probably on account of the expense, and it was to be another twelve years before his name was again put forward – this time without his knowledge. He accepted the honour. Meanwhile in 1817 he had been elected as president of the Manchester Literary and Philosophical Society and he held that post up until the end of his life.

If Dalton had achieved nothing else, he would still have justified a reputation as a thorough and competent scientist, but his claim to fame was his atomic theory, and his proposition of a table of atomic weights in particular. This was first set out in his book *A New System of Chemical Philosophy*, published in 1808.

The idea of everything being made up of atoms was not new – it had been proposed by the ancient Greeks, but it was a theory which had fallen out of favour. Dalton gave new impetus to the idea, and thereby laid the foundations for modern chemistry. His theory included these points:

1. *Elements are made of extremely small particles called atoms.*
2. *Atoms of a given element are identical in size, mass and other properties;*
3. *Atoms of different elements differ in size, mass and other properties.*
4. *Atoms cannot be subdivided, created or destroyed.*
5. *Atoms of different elements combine in simple whole-number ratios to form chemical compounds.*
6. *In chemical reactions, atoms are combined, separated or rearranged.*

There have, of course, been adjustments made to these rules – not least by the splitting of the atom, and of the discovery that a single element can have several isotopes. But the basic concept provided a framework for understanding how compounds could be made. Suddenly, scientists had a logical explanation for the way elements combined. It was a concept which Dalton brought to life by demonstrating his theory with a number of spherical shapes which could be linked to other spheres by using a differing numbers of metal rods. He also illustrated his papers with the first table of atomic weights, showing each different element as a differently marked circle. His proposal divided the scientific community and initially Dalton had to put up with considerable ridicule and criticism. However, in time his brilliant and simple explanation won over his critics, both in Britain and abroad.

John Dalton was a man of simple tastes; he never bothered to buy his own house, and stayed as a lodger with his friends, the Revd William Johns and his wife, at their home in Manchester's George Street for thirty years. Earlier, when he first went to Manchester, he happily used the College premises as his living quarters, as well as for all of his studies. He enjoyed the company of women, but never married, offering the oft-repeated claim that 'he never had time'. He was a creature of habit, always playing bowls on a Thursday evening at the Dog and Partridge public house. Ever meticulous, he even recorded his scores on each occasion he played. In the environment of the lecture theatre he was not an inspiring figure, being described by one of his contemporaries as a 'tall, gaunt, awkward scholar'. He was, however, an able coach and mentor on a one-to-one basis, and there was an occasion when a visiting French dignitary was astonished to find the old man instructing a 10-year-old boy in simple arithmetic. On other occasions his pupils included James Prescott Joule, who later went on to formulate the first law of thermo-dynamics.

Even though he enjoyed an international reputation for his theories on atomic weights, he never grew rich on the back of his achievements and even into his sixties was compelled to give private coaching in arithmetic to paying pupils. This alarmed his friends to the extent that they petitioned the government for a pension, and finally the government of Earl Grey awarded a pension of £150 a year. This was doubled in 1836. Just to put such largesse in context: the courtesan Elizabeth Armistead, former mistress to the Prince of Wales (later George IV) was, at much the same time, given a pension of £1,200 per annum.

In time, Dalton headed the scientific community in Manchester, cementing its reputation as a leading scientific centre outside London. He gave lectures across the country, notably in Leeds, Edinburgh and Glasgow. He always valued his independence from 'the London set', and when the inaugural meeting of the British Association was held in York in 1831, he urged members to hold all subsequent meetings away from London, in order to encourage scientific endeavour throughout the provinces. He attended subsequent meetings of the Association in Bristol, Oxford and Dublin.

From 1816 he had been a corresponding member of the French Académie des Sciences, and in 1830 was elected as one of its eight foreign associates. Four years earlier he had been awarded the Royal Society's Gold Medal. He was also elected a Foreign Honorary Member of the American Academy of Arts and Sciences in 1834. More awards included doctorates from both Oxford and Edinburgh Universities, and he enjoyed the rare distinction (possibly even unique, for a scientist) of having a statue erected in his honour in his lifetime when a sculpture by Francis Leggatt Chantrey, showing Dalton wearing his full academic robes, was erected in the vestibule of Manchester's Town Hall.

In his biography on John Dalton in the Oxford Dictionary of National Biography, Frank Greenaway ends with the words:

His intellectual legacy remains: he was one of the first of the modern type of professional scientist, the man who combines the study of the external world with the duty to instruct and with his own need to gain a livelihood. Without any help from the great universities, the established church, or the wealth of an old-established family, he made, on his own, a career in which he brought about as profound a change in the nature of physical science as any one man has ever done.

It makes it all the more surprising that in the intervening years since his death, his achievements have faded into the background. Of course, he is still well known in the scientific community, but in general those 40,000 ordinary Mancunians who turned up to see him lie in state have been replaced by a populace who have completely forgotten him. We may read about Michael Faraday and his experiments with electro-magnetism; we may be reminded about the relevance and achievements of Joseph Priestley; we may know about Humphry Davy (without being quite sure why); but, in general, we have forgotten the unassuming John Dalton. However, it has to be said: Dalton would never have wanted fame, posthumous or otherwise. He would probably be content just to know that many of his ideas are still accepted and respected by other scientists. To him, what mattered was imparting knowledge to the next generation, and it is something he did quietly, effectively and without a trace of pomposity. As Sir Humphry Davy (a man who had initially mocked Dalton's theories) said of him:

Mr Dalton's permanent reputation will rest upon his having discovered a simple principle, universally applicable to the facts of chemistry – in fixing the proportions in which bodies combine, and thus laying the foundations for future labours.

John Bird, 1709–1776

The eighteenth century saw an astonishing boom in Britain's trade with the rest of the world – and the nation's ships were at the heart of the trade bonanza which led to the emergence of the British Empire. And what the owners and operators of merchant ships wanted more than anything else was the answer to the question: where exactly are we?

Time and again ships were lost because of inaccurate charts and because navigators were unable to calculate a ship's position in relation to hidden rocks, shoals and sandbanks. The Board of Longitude (more properly, the Commissioners for the Discovery of the Longitude at Sea) had been formed in 1714 to administer a scheme of prizes intended to encourage innovators to solve the problem of finding longitude at sea. The challenge was duly taken up by astronomers, who worked on solving the conundrum using lunar tables, as well as by instrument workers who sought a mechanical solution. Much credit is nowadays given to John Harrison and his marine chronometer, but it is worth putting his success in perspective: by the end of the Georgian period Harrison's marine chronometers were not in general use in the navy, whereas lunar tables, developed by Tobias Meyer, were universally used.

To use the lunar tables you first had to have accurate measurements – traditionally done by instruments such as the quadrant or octant. Tobias Meyer himself experimented with a repeating circle, made of wood, and in 1756 sea trials were carried out off Finisterre by Captain John Campbell, a Royal Navy navigational expert, on board HMS *Essex*. Earlier, Campbell had been one of the first to experiment with Hadley's octant, one of many devices put forward as a means of measuring distances between different objects. The octant had first appeared in 1731 and had the drawback of only measuring up to forty-five degrees.

This time around Campbell found that the circular instrument was far too bulky and heavy, and that only a third of the scale was usable. Campbell recommended that a London instrument maker by the name of John Bird should be asked to come up with a device called a sextant, made of brass rather than wood, and having a radius double that of the repeating circle. Bird's instrument, trialled off the coast of Ushant by Campbell on board HMS *Royal George* in 1759, was a great success. James Bradley, the Astronomer Royal, checked the measurements and found them to be spot-on. The sextant was lighter – just one third the weight of the reflective circle – and had a smaller arc of 60 degrees.

Why had Campbell chosen Bird? Because he had a reputation for preparing gauges of incredible accuracy. The principle behind the sextant was not new, as it developed out of ideas put forward by Sir Isaac Newton fifty years earlier. Newton had suggested the use of double reflection in 1699. The sextant had an arc of 60 degrees – a sixth of a whole circle – and incorporated a telescope and a circular glass, the lower half of which was mirrored, with the reflected element displayed on to a second mirror. By altering the angle of that second mirror the object being looked at – for instance the midday sun – could be lowered to the line of the horizon. It was a device which enabled the viewer to see the object – the sun – and the horizon all on one level, through one eye. The angle could then be read off and the reading could then be applied to make sense of the lunar tables.

The sextant worked on the principle that a reflected ray of light leaves a plane surface at the same angle at which it strikes the surface – in scientific terms, 'the angle of reflection is equal to the angle of incidence'. It also follows the principle that 'two reflective planes or mirrors create an angle of inclination which, through logic and transposition, when doubled, equals the altitude of the celestial body'. In layman's terms, if the gauge measuring the angle was correct, it could give the user very accurate measurements of the distance between any two objects.

The sextant had many advantages over anything previously in use. Unlike the quadrant, it could measure angles up to 120 degrees, which made it ideal for measuring the angle between the sun and the moon. It could be used both in daylight and at night, and this meant it could be used for measuring distances from the stars. Measuring the distance between the moon and the stars enabled the user to determine Greenwich Mean Time. The sextant's ability to bring the two images in line helped iron out any problems caused by the movement of the ship – indeed the aim of the operator and the steadiness of the ship was not material, because the horizon and the planets, or other celestial object being looked at, remained steady in their relative positions. The ship might move, but the objects did not.

It required no power source, which is one reason why, even in today's age with GPS, sextants are still in use. It also explains why the Orion Space probe, being developed by the Lockheed Martin Corporation and intended for use in exploring Mars, will have on board a sextant which incorporates many of the features of the John Bird prototype. Back in the eighteenth century, the sextant may have been more expensive than the quadrant, but it was far better made and calibrated, and was soon brought into common use. From the second-half of the century onwards, every single one of the important voyages of discovery used a sextant, from James Cook to Matthew Flinders, from William Bligh to Nicholas Baudin and Louis-Antoine de Bougainville.

So, who was Bird? He was born and baptised in Bishop Auckland in the northeast of England in 1709. He appears to have been apprenticed as a weaver, but the story goes that he was intrigued at finding a longcase clock with inaccurate divisions on its dials. He experimented with marking the dials in a more precise fashion and soon developed this into a profitable sideline. His skill in dividing circles and engraving these divisions onto brass developed, and by 1740 he felt able to move to London to gain work as an instrument maker, working for Jonathan Sissons. Here, under the sign of the Sphere, at Beaufort Buildings in London's Strand, he was able to observe Sissons make theodolites and astronomical instruments such as mural quadrants. These massive metal structures involved a telescope mounted on a quarter-circle frame, fixed to a wall aligned north-south so that the two sides run vertical and horizontal.

While working for Sissons he met George Graham, a renowned clockmaker. Graham gave assistance to Bird, enabling him to open his own business in 1745. By then he was 36 years old, quite late to be developing such a specialist business. He operated from premises at the sign of the Sea Quadrant, Strand, and quickly became renowned for quality and accuracy. Within three years he was approached by James Bradley, the Astronomer Royal, to build a mural quadrant at Greenwich, 8ft across. The contract also involved recalibrating the observatory's existing mural quadrant. Bird's success led to commissions from other observatories, including those in St Petersburg, Cadiz and Paris. Subsequently, he received a commission from the Radcliffe Observatory in Oxford. This project involved two mural quadrants – work which was to take Bird the rest of his life.

In the 1760s Bird wrote two books, the first published in 1767 being *The Method of Dividing Astronomic Instruments*, followed the next year by *The Method of Constructing a Mural Quadrant*. In doing this he was departing from the more traditional secrecy which was a feature of so many instrument makers. In part, his openness was a result of having been paid £500 by the Longitude Board. This was conditional upon him being transparent with his methods, and also upon him agreeing to take on apprentices nominated by the Board. The payment was intended to enable Bird to open new premises, needed so he could make further instruments for the Board. In the past, these had included portable astronomical instruments used during the trials of John Harrison's marine timekeepers.

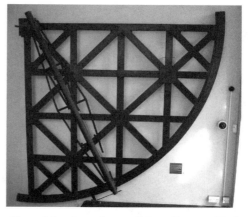

Bird was increasingly having difficulties keeping up with demand; fulfilling orders was taking not months but years. His health started to deteriorate and he died, at the age of 66, on 31 March 1776. Under his Will he appointed John Campbell as one of his joint executors and left him his gold watch and half his estate.

Above: Mural quadrant; *Below*: Sextant. Both made by John Bird.

It can be argued that Bird was simply one of many makers of scientific instruments which required great accuracy and detail. But in developing the world's first working sextant, he transformed navigation at sea – to a far greater extent than many of his more famous contemporaries. It is only now, 250 years later with the arrival of GPS, that his instrument has been overtaken.

Chapter 7

Entertainment and the Arts

An image from Astley's book on equestrian training.

Philip Astley, 1742–1814

Few nowadays are familiar with the name of Philip Astley. Some may know him as 'the Father of the Modern Circus', but few appreciate what this self-made man achieved and how important he is to the whole history of mass entertainment – and to variety shows in particular.

His was a remarkable success story of the eighteenth century – an entrepreneur who established a name for himself both in England and Europe; a businessman who bounced back even when fire repeatedly destroyed his premises; a real showman, and a larger-than-life character. He was tall and powerfully built – you would not have been able to miss *him* in a crowded room!

Born in Newcastle-under-Lyme in 1742, he had a very limited education and was expected to follow in his father's footsteps as a cabinet maker. This involved repetitive and tedious work, indoors, selecting and matching veneers in his father's carpentry shop. He hated the work – and he was constantly arguing with his father. The pair never got on. When he turned 17 he knew exactly what he wanted – he wanted to work outdoors, with horses. He wanted excitement, he wanted to travel, and for him that meant joining the Fifteenth Light Dragoons.

He saw action almost immediately when his unit was sent to Flanders at the start of the Seven Years War. He learned how to break in young horses, how to train and discipline them, how to feed and care for them. Above all, while he was in the army Astley's job had been to train the horses for battle – to make them utterly reliable and 'bomb proof'. His dedication turned him into something of a legend in the army – he was the 'Horse Whisperer' of the Age. Indeed, later in his life he published a book, the 1801 *Astleys System of Equestrian Education*. At the end of the text the author styles himself 'Philip Astley, professor of the Art of Riding'. Modesty never was his strong point!

Astley had a distinguished army career – once, during the Seven Years War, he single-handedly captured an enemy standard at the battle of Emsdorf. On another occasion he personally rescued the Duke of Brunswick, who was injured and had fallen behind enemy lines. Astley charged through the line, picked up the wounded duke, and carried him back to safety. Not a bad person to have as an indebted friend – the duke was married to the sister of George III.

Astley was decorated and rose through the ranks to become sergeant major. With his imposing physique and bellowing voice he must have fitted the role perfectly. When he left the army as a 24-year-old in June 1766, he was presented with a white charger named Gibraltar by Baron Heathfield, the general in charge of his unit. On Gibraltar, he trotted off to London, determined to make his fortune by teaching equestrian skills to others, and by giving displays of trick riding. From such humble beginnings an empire was born...

At first, Astley worked for a Mr and Mrs Sampson, who ran a riding school in Islington in a paddock at the back of the Three Hats Public house, near Astley's lodgings. For some years the Sampsons had earned a living teaching horse-riding and demonstrating tricks. The area had a tradition of showing equestrian acts, and a number of booths and observation boxes encircled the riding area. Quite possibly it was this ring of structures which inspired Astley's later experiments with a circular arena.

After a year, Astley decided to branch out on his own and give riding lessons himself, using the pupils to 'put on a bit of a show' in the afternoon. He leased a field in Lambeth called 'Glovers Halfpenny Hatch', and gave riding lessons in the morning and demonstrations of equestrian skills in the afternoon. A bucket would be passed round as a collection after the show, and before long the profits enabled Astley to employ a couple of musicians to bang a drum and play the fiddle.

It looks as though Lady Luck was shining on Philip Astley – by now married to a girl called Patty. The story goes that one day, near Westminster Bridge, they found a diamond ring. No one claimed it, and Astley sold it for £60 – a rather large sum of money. The story sounds slightly improbable, and it was first rolled out when a rival suggested that Astley had come by his money dishonestly. Astley countered with the story of the diamond ring, which must have been a real sparkler to have been worth that amount of money. Wherever it came from, Astley used some of the money to buy a pony called 'Billy' for his wife. No ordinary pony this, for it became known as 'The Little Military Learned Horse' — he trained it to add and subtract numbers (or rather, pretend to do so by scraping a hoof over the ground the appropriate number of times), feign death, fire a pistol, and perform 'mind-reading' tricks, and Billy went on to become famous in his own right, appearing in performances for over forty years.

On 6 April 1768, Philip Astley's name first appeared in the London newspapers under the small heading 'Activity on horseback'; four lines of text advertised that he would perform upwards of twenty 'attitudes' on one, two and three horses at the New Spring Gardens in Chelsea. Admission cost 1 shilling.

The Astleys would ride two horses together, one foot on each animal, firing pistols, jumping into the air, or leaping through hoops before landing again on the back of the horses. Another trick was doing a headstand, on horseback, while firing a pistol. Trick riding, and training a horse to do party tricks by appearing to add or count cards was nothing new, but Astley developed it into a totally different form of entertainment.

In those early days Patty also had her own act, in which she appeared on the back of 'Billy', while her arms and hands were covered with a swarm of bees so thick that it resembled a ladies muff. Patty was a very striking woman, with hair over 5ft long which hung straight to the ground. One day it caught fire, and after that she wore her hair wound up in a huge net worn on top of her head, causing one member of the audience to remark that it was like watching a whale appear on stage.

Early on, Astley started to work on one particular act, called the Tailor of Brentford. Dressed as a clown called Billy Buttons, Astley would run up and attempt to mount his horse, which would step backwards at the critical moment, leaving the hapless clown flat on his face. The routine would be repeated over again and eventually the rider ended up on the horse's back, but facing the wrong way and would fall off. One moment the horse would refuse to move, and the next he would be chased around the ring by Astley the clown. The horse would pick up speed until he was the one chasing after the clown. The routine continued until finally the horse would kneel. Astley would climb onto the horse's back and at last he would stop clowning and reveal himself as the superb rider he really was. The crowd loved it, and the slapstick element of the act can be traced through the centuries, right up until the likes of Buster Keaton.

This was the first time ever that clowning had been combined with horse riding. Back in the early 1770s, Astley's bumbling impersonation of a gaudily dressed tailor trying to ride a horse caused great hilarity. Apparently, on one occasion, a tailor in the audience complained that it was a slur on his profession – the tailor was accordingly invited to come and ride for the benefit of the audience. Little did he know that as soon as he was mounted, one click of Astley's fingers and the horse dropped to its knees, launching the hapless tailor headfirst into the sawdust. It proved so popular that this 'spontaneous' audience involvement became a regular feature.

The combination of clowning and equestrian skills became immensely popular and was soon a feature of all the copycat circus venues which quickly sprang up. In time, Astley trained other riders to take his place as clown and he concentrated on the one role which he created for himself – that of the ringmaster.

Success enabled Astley to travel the country with touring shows appearing in wooden amphitheatres – they became so popular he was given the derogatory nickname of 'Amphi-Philip'. He settled on a ring with a diameter of 42ft – the smallest turning circle for a horse galloping at full speed and at which the rider could rely on centrifugal force to keep himself upright on the horses back. It is still the standard size of circus ring in use today.

For weeks at a time Astley would be on the road, to places such as Norwich, Stamford, Leeds, Manchester, and even up to Edinburgh. Sometimes he headed west, to Oxford, Bath and on to Bristol. Wherever he went, he made sure that the newspapers carried stories of his extraordinary feats of horse riding – he really was a brilliant self-publicist, the Richard Branson of the age. His travelling shows were like a Royal Progress – waggon after waggon of gaudily painted props and staging materials, preceded by the horses themselves being ridden into town with full military pomp and splendour.

It is worth remembering that basing the entertainment on equestrian skills made it relevant and available to the entire audience – even if people did not own a horse, their world revolved around the horse – horses drew wagons and coaches, carts and carriages. Before the Industrial Revolution, in manufacturing businesses and in mining, horsepower was exactly that – the power of the horse. Hence people could identify with the skill needed to make a horse perform tricks.

Astley settled into a habit of giving performances in London from Easter through until September, when he would then go off on tour until the following spring. The money started to flow in. But Astley aspired to more than performing in an open field before a small crowd – he wanted the big time, and that meant decent premises. In 1769, Astley secured the lease of a former sawmill premises on the corner of Stangate Street and Westminster Bridge Road – highly visible premises, right on a popular thoroughfare. A wooden structure was put up to shelter the crowds from the wind, but it was still roofless and therefore subject to the vagaries of an English summer.

Astley drew inspiration from the legitimate theatre – where managers were forever adding visual treats to try and build up public interest and 'put bums on seats'. Indeed, it had reached the stage where David Garrick, the great Shakespearian actor of the day, had remarked that adding jugglers and rope walkers was a sacrilege: 'nothing but downright starving would induce me to bring such defilement and abomination to the house of William Shakespeare.'

Astley had no such scruples. Although there was no blueprint to work from, he experimented by adding together visual performances which traditionally had been seen as separate entertainments. So, just as he did not invent clowning but added it to riding skills, so he added what were previously fairground entertainments – juggling, slack-wire walking, acrobatics and feats of strength such as the human pyramid – to give the public the chance to see a whole range of skills, all on the same entrance ticket. Astley added conjuring tricks, mind-reading tricks, and novelty acts such as performing dogs. Arguably, modern variety shows all share the same common ancestry.

The only thing Astley did <u>not</u> do was add wild animals – because to him it was the training which was central. It is therefore ironic that in the past fifty years the modern circus has fallen out of favour because of its association with acts involving animals such as lions and elephants – creatures which Astley would never have considered using. Instead he used dogs, a monkey called General Jacko, and even a performing pig as novelty items between the main horse-riding exhibitions.

Astley really was, through and through, a showman. He used fireworks, he used an orchestra, and he showed his military background by dressing everything in his favourite colours – red and gold. By adding music to these equestrian skills, plus all the variety acts, he created a new style of popular entertainment. Before Astley, there really was no mass entertainment suitable for the whole family, apart from fairs and travelling shows. The theatres were dens of immorality, with much raucous and unseemly behaviour unsuitable for children. Astley's blueprint for a show which would appeal to rich and poor alike, which crossed all social boundaries and which appealed to both young and old, became incredibly popular in a very short period of time.

When Astley's son John was 5 years old he appeared on horseback on stage – and went on to become a hugely popular performer. He was as good a rider as his parents. Astley trained pairs of horses to pirouette in time to the music – to appear as if dancing the minuet. He also trained Patty's horse Billy to loosen its own girth and to remove its saddle. The horse would then saunter over to a kettle and appear to pour himself a cup of tea.

For the jugglers, tumblers and contortionists, Astley and his circus must have been a godsend, because life had not been easy for street entertainers since the introduction of the Licensing Act of 1737. The legislation stated that street entertainers were liable to be treated as vagabonds – at best moved on to the next parish, at worst fined and thrown in prison. Astley offered them employment and a chance to spend a whole season in one place – but he himself had numerous run-ins with the magistrates. Fortunately, he always seemed to know someone who would bail him out and have a word with the magistrate, and there is a suggestion that the 'someone' was none other than George III, who was a fervent admirer of Astley. Indeed, he was frequently asked by the monarch to come and give demonstrations of his riding skills. Having friends in high places certainly helped keep Astley in the news – but out of prison.

Astley developed a number of different routines, which would be changed every fortnight, so that hopefully the public could be persuaded to come and see the show on more than one occasion. And when news of the death of Captain Cook in far off Hawaii filtered back to England, Astley immediately put on his version of the battle between the British landing party and the perfidious natives, who attacked and killed Cook on 14 February 1783. The fact that horses were conspicuous by their absence in Hawaii was neither here nor there – and the audiences loved it!

Astley was never backwards in coming forwards to promote the business, and would lead a procession through the streets of Westminster ahead of the show, with trumpeters and drummers literally drumming up business. He was also fiercely patriotic and frequently marked the king's birthday by floating on his back from Blackfriars Bridge to Westminster Bridge, holding a flag in each hand, waving at the passers-by, or by giving special firework displays; he was a one-man publicity machine. Within months of the first balloon ascent by the Montgolfier brothers in 1783, he had sponsored an ascent from the amphitheatre premises – one of the first balloon flights in England.

Success always brings copycats, in this case a showman named Hughes who, in 1772, opened rival premises on Blackfriars Road, just a few yards away from Astley. Hughes had originally been taught by Astley, but the two men had parted on bad terms and Astley felt that the young upstart was not showing him enough respect. Hughes openly mocked Astley for his poor education, and reckoned that anything Astley could do, he could do better. For a couple of years the pair battled it out, with some splendid 'knocking copy' advertisements. Competition was of course great for business.

Pressure from the legitimate theatres at Covent Garden and Drury Lane led to both sets of circus premises being closed in July 1773 because neither had a performing licence. Astley's rival Hughes then set off on an eight-year-long European tour, which included opening a circus in St Petersburg at the request of the Imperial Court, leaving the London scene to Astley. Soon Astley was able to secure a licence, supposedly as a result of saving King George III from a riding accident on Westminster Bridge.

Towards the end of 1778 Astley could afford to add a roof to the premises, enabling him to put on shows throughout the winter months. He was also able to give evening performances, to the intense annoyance of the legitimate London Theatres, with whom he was now in direct competition. Astley reopened his premises in January 1779 under a new name, 'Astley's Royal Grove and Amphitheatre Riding House'.

He went on to open permanent premises in Dublin, Brussels, Vienna, and Belgrade. In all he was to build nineteen circus premises throughout Europe – although he always called them 'amphitheatres'. He also decided to open premises in Paris, but one problem he had to face was that French licensing controls meant Astley could only get a licence if he could show the authorities that his acts were different to anything else on the Parisian stage at the time. When he was told that his entertainment was permitted as long as 'the entire show was on horseback', he is reported to have complied by balancing the staging for the acrobats on the backs of the horses standing underneath.

Astley didn't have London all to himself for long. Hughes returned from his highly successful tour of the Continent in 1781 and began building a brand-new amphitheatre, this time in stone. Once again, Hughes chose premises right on the doorstep of Astley's amphitheatre, next to a well-known landmark with an obelisk in its centre known as St George's Circus. Hughes applied the name 'circus' to his actual premises, and modestly called them 'The Royal Circus', and it opened in November 1782. The animosity between Astley and Hughes had intensified when Astley fell out with his elderly father (not for the first time) and kicked him out on the streets. Hughes immediately employed Astley Senior as a bill-sticker, putting up advertisements for the Hughes circus. Astley Junior was incandescent.

Not only was the Hughes building the first modern amphitheatre to bear the title 'circus', but it combined a fully equipped theatre stage and a circus ring. The stage-and-ring arrangement introduced by Hughes became standard for nearly all circus buildings for the next seventy-five years – and Astley quickly took note. When Astley refurbished his premises in 1786, he included a theatre stage next to the ring, and eventually fought off the competition. His rival was constantly embroiled in financial feuds and litigation, but eventually Hughes died, and his partner went bankrupt. In time the Hughes circus premises became a legitimate theatre.

When the storming of the Bastille took place on 14 July 1789, Astley presented a re-enactment on stage almost before the month was out. It heralded a tradition of putting on re-enactments of famous battles, sieges and naval victories which lasted well into the Victorian era. More and more elaborate recreations of battle scenes were performed, with cannon on stage, horses dramatically jumping from platform to stage to circus ring, and with pyrotechnics and loud bangs keeping the audiences on the edge of their seats.

Meanwhile, one of Hughes pupils by the name of John Bill Ricketts headed for America, and in April 1793 he opened the very first American circus, in Philadelphia. Ricketts became a friend of George Washington, and used his connections to become a highly popular entertainer.

Back in Europe, Astley continued to face obstacles – the French Revolution meant that he had to hand over control of his Paris amphitheatre to an Italian businessman, and his Parisian stables were commandeered by the French army. Also, his Dublin premises were badly affected by sectarian unrest and rioting. In 1793, war with France broke out and the 51-year-old Astley re-enlisted with the Fifteenth Light Dragoons, but came out from the army a year later when his Westminster Bridge premises were totally destroyed by fire. Such fires were commonplace – small wonder with naked candles being used in the footlights and overhead candelabra, with straw and sawdust on the floor, and with the staging and seating all made of old wood. Astley's building was seriously under-insured and the majority of the rebuilding costs – running to many thousands of pounds – had to come from Astley's pocket. Astonishingly, Astley was able to rebuild from scratch and reopen by Easter 1795, and this gives some idea of how profitable these entertainments had become.

Indeed, it is his resilience, his determination, and his nerves of steel which made him such a durable success. This time, when he rebuilt the amphitheatre he added ramps so that horses and riders could move from the circus ring up to the stage, considerably adding to the theatrical effect. One of his first acts was to announce that all members of the armed forces would be given front row seats, free of charge, a simple patriotic gesture which greatly enhanced his popularity.

Philip had started to take a back seat, leaving more of the day-to-day business to his son John. In 1799 he more-or-less retired to concentrate on writing his treatise on horse management, and he transferred a half share in the business to John. But retirement was not to last long. In 1802 peace with France meant that Astley, then 60 years of age, was able to travel to France in what appeared to be a forlorn attempt to persuade the French government to pay him compensation for the loss of his business. Amazingly, he met the Emperor Napoleon and persuaded him to return property to the value of £10,000 – and to pay him back-rent, amounting to a total of £14,000, for the past ten years. However, peace with France was short lived; in 1803 Astley failed to get out of the country in time and, as an enemy subject, was thrown in prison. With typical daring and courage, Astley pretended to be ill and conned the authorities into granting him free passage to the spa town of Montpellier. He reportedly hijacked the coach transporting him there and instead rode hell-for-leather to the German border, escaping down the Rhine. It was only then that he heard the devastating news that his wife Patty had died on 25 August. More bad news was to follow; one week later his amphitheatre in London caught fire yet again and was totally destroyed. His son John also lost his mother-in-law in the blaze.

Once more the amphitheatre was rebuilt, with an even more ornate design, and was in use for the 1805 season. Meanwhile in the same year Philip Astley had obtained a licence to build yet another amphitheatre, this time in the Strand. He built it using the salvaged timbers from an old French warship, and called the premises the Olympic Pavilion. It opened in September 1806, but try as he might, Astley was unable to make this new circus pay. He lost a small fortune on the venture, which was eventually sold in 1813.

John earned a fortune with what became known as 'hippo-dramas'. One particular production written and produced by John in 1810 called *The Blood-Red Knight or The Fatal Bridge*, reportedly earned the amphitheatre profits of £18,000 in a single year – a vast amount of money.

When he turned 70, Philip Astley retired to live in Paris. His place in the ring had been taken by a brilliant Belgian rider called Ducrow – if anything, the best rider of them all. Astley died in 1814 in Paris, with the obituary in the *Gentleman's Magazine* giving the cause of death as 'gout in the stomach'. By a strange quirk of fate his son died in the same bed in the same room just seven years later. Both father and son were buried in the same Parisian cemetery. Apparently, son John's gravestone bore the inscription 'the English rose' – the name given him by Marie Antoinette, who had showered father and son with awards and jewels before she was carted off to the guillotine. No trace of either of the Astley graves remains.

Astley's inspiration led to the circus becoming a worldwide phenomenon. In 1825, the American Joshuah Purdy Brown became the first circus entrepreneur to replace the usual wooden structure with a full canvas tent. He went into partnership with a man called Hachaliah Bailey, who just happened to own a bull elephant, and together they pioneered the idea of a travelling, tented, menagerie. By the 1830s the tented enclosures were the norm in America – and in time the idea crossed back to Britain.

Eventually the American version, concentrating on wild animals rather than on horse-riding skills, predominated, and the whole character of the circus changed forever. By the end of the Victorian era P.T. Barnum was posing the question: 'why give the public a minnow when you can give them a whale?' Accordingly, he brought on stage not one, but a dozen lions and tigers; not one, but a score of elephants.

Back in England Ducrow took over as manager, and the circus prospered until 1841 when fire again destroyed the amphitheatre. Ducrow suffered a complete nervous and physical breakdown as a result of the fire, and died shortly afterwards. Once more the premises rose from the ashes, and a succession of managers followed, before the premises finally closed in 1893. The venue was demolished two years later, and the nurses' accommodation block at St Thomas's Hospital now stands on the original site.

By the time it closed, the Astley name had been associated with an incredibly popular and accessible form of public entertainment for over one hundred years. But however popular and instantly recognisable he may have been in his lifetime, Astley left barely any trace of his success. There are no blue plaques in Lambeth recording where Astley lived, there are no pubs bearing his name, and there are no Astley Streets in London named after him. The nearest we get is a Hercules Street in Lambeth, named after Astley's human pyramid.

He was a populist, a charismatic figure and a brilliant showman. He may have been a poorly educated, blunt-speaking, bully of a man, but he deserves to be remembered for his enormous contribution to popular entertainment.

Joseph Wright of Derby, 1734–1797

Painting came a long way in the Georgian period, moving on from the rather rigid three-quarter length portraits by Sir Godfrey Kneller, in the reign of Queen Anne, to the soft, almost intimate, portraits by Sir Thomas Lawrence in the Regency era. Landscape artists such as Constable and Turner showed new ways of observing the world outside the drawing rooms of the rich and famous, while artists such as William Blake rebelled against the teaching of Sir Joshua Reynolds. Reynolds thought that artists should concentrate on pursuing what was called 'general truth' and 'general beauty'.

In practice this had meant that 'serious' paintings were expected to follow classical precedents – especially those with religious themes. Biblical stories had dominated the art world for centuries, which makes the work of a man called Joseph Wright all the more remarkable. He showed wonderment in his pictures, not in terms of a religious experience, but in terms of the changes brought about by the discoveries which tumbled forth during the Industrial Revolution. He showed onlookers gaping in amazement at scientific experiments, and captured a world in which change was profoundly altering society. He was the artist of the Industrial Revolution, and he worked close to the heart of where that revolution took place – the Midlands.

In particular, he was closely associated with many of the members of the Lunar Society, and is especially remembered for his painting of Erasmus Darwin, featured earlier and shown in Plate 10.

Joseph Wright was born in September 1734 in the Irongate district of Derby, the third of five children born to Hannah Wright. She was the wife of John, a local lawyer who operated as Derby's Town Clerk. Joseph Wright was educated at Derby Grammar School and showed an early interest in drawing, copying existing prints, and teaching himself by doing studies of hands and faces. In 1751 the 17-year-old moved to London to learn under the auspices of Thomas Hudson, a renowned portrait artist of the period who had taught Joshua Reynolds ten years previously.

After a couple of years, Wright returned to Derby and experimented with painting local scenes and local people, but he appears to have lacked confidence and within three years returned to work as Thomas Hudson's assistant. He remained in London for fifteen months before turning his back on London and heading home to Derby. In time, his attachment to the city was what earned him the soubriquet Joseph Wright 'of Derby', but this also helped distinguish him from other artists of the same name. In particular he sought to avoid confusion with Joseph, the son of the wax modeller Patience Wright, who had been admitted to the Royal Academy school of painting in 1775; he too went on to become a portrait painter, although in his case he went to America to pursue his painting career and established a name for himself designing coins for use in the United States in the aftermath of the American Revolution.

'Joseph Wright of Derby' fully deserves his description – he was Midlands through and through. He painted the people he knew, and they felt relaxed in the company of someone who knew them, knew their importance locally, knew their aspirations and was unfettered by notions of following whatever was fashionable at the time in London. He started to exhibit paintings at the Society of Artists in 1769 and at the Royal Academy in various years between 1778 and 1794. However, a great change occurred in July 1773 when, at the age of 39, he married the daughter of a local lead miner, a girl called Ann (otherwise known as Hannah). Little is known about her, but Wright's own niece Hannah described her as 'a person in an inferior situation of life'. She became pregnant immediately, but this did not stop the pair heading off on a tour of Italy in November 1773 with a couple of friends – a tour which lasted over eighteen months until the Wright family set off for home in June 1775, reaching Derby in September of that year. By then their daughter, Anna Romana, was over a year old. The couple went on to have six children, with three of them reaching adulthood.

Wright's time in Italy was spent mainly in Rome drawing antiquities, and also in Naples and the Bay of Salerno. It was a visit which obviously inspired Wright and he painted many pictures of Vesuvius erupting – even though there were actually no real eruptions occurring during the period of his stay. Nevertheless, he would have observed the lava flows and been aware of the enormous power of volcanic activity. He was fascinated by light and raw power – forces which he also identified in many of his later studies of industrial subjects.

Returning to England, Wright headed for Bath, following in the footsteps of Thomas Gainsborough. He presumably thought that he too could find success by painting the portraits of the fun-seeking aristocrats and wealthy merchants heading for 'the season' at the spa resort. He was to be disappointed. Like a fish out of water, he returned to his beloved Derby, and remained there from 1777 until his death twenty years later. He painted the people he knew and could relate to – the mill owners, the industrialists, the movers and shakers of the local community.

He became a master of using shade and light, specialising in pictures lit from one side by candlelight, giving strong shadows. It was a style known as chiaroscuro, and he used it to illustrate many of his science-based paintings – for instance his *Experiment on a Bird in an Air-Pump* painted in 1768. Two years earlier, he had produced *A Philosopher Lecturing on the Orrery* – a startlingly powerful portrayal of a lecturer demonstrating an orrery, showing the movement of the planets around the sun. It is shown in Plate 8. The central sun has been represented by a lantern, which casts its shadows over the faces of the eager onlookers. Some observers were outraged that the wonderment and awe reserved for religious paintings had been hijacked in this way – it was a sort of parody which made many people feel uncomfortable. To Wright it was not in any way heretical – simply an expression of the battle between science and religion which marked the Age of Enlightenment.

Joseph Wright's wife Ann died on 17 August 1790. He soldiered on for another seven years, increasingly suffering from asthma and what was termed dropsy – (nowadays, oedema, i.e. an abnormal accumulation of fluid). He was a patient of Erasmus Darwin and, despite the good doctor's ministrations, died at his home at 26 Queen Street, Derby, on 29 August 1797. Following his death he was buried in St Alkmund's Church, Derby, in a churchyard which was later demolished to make way for a bypass. His body was reinterred in Nottingham Road Cemetery and the tombstone was re-erected in Derby Cathedral.

The city of Derby is justifiably proud of Wright, and there is a particularly extensive collection of his paintings in the City Art Gallery.

James Gillray, 1756–1815

Gillray deserves a place as a Georgian Great because he pioneered a change which has echoed down the centuries, continued by the likes of Spitting Image and the works of caricaturists such as Gerald Scarfe. His métier was parody – laced with acerbic wit. In some ways he was a ball of bile – a twisted, angry, criticising dynamo. He railed against the rich; he railed against the poor. He mocked the French; he mocked the Irish; he mocked the Scots and when it suited him, he mocked the English. He savaged government policy and government ministers, just as he ridiculed the opposition. He skated close to seditious libel with his criticism of the king, and yet somehow managed to avoid being charged with criminal libel. He could be witty, he could be cruel, but above all he made people laugh, especially at their elders and betters. No one was safe from his critical penmanship – and he was perfectly willing to sell his soul to whoever was prepared to pay for his talents. His humour was often of the schoolboy, lavatorial, variety – and he loved puns. But he also had the ability to shock – and to inform. An example is shown in Plate 3, where he likens the plantation owner to a cannibal devouring the bodies of slaves.

He was not, of course, the first to use satire – Hogarth preceded him in many ways, but Hogarth was a finger-wagging moralist in comparison with Gillray. Hogarth was meticulously accurate, almost architecturally so. The perspective in his drawings was always right, his criticism always controlled and reasoned, but he also lacked the verve, the spirit, the sheer mischievous joy of life which imbued the works of Gillray.

And because of his scatter-gun approach, he was loved even by the people he sometimes targeted – even the Prince of Wales collected his caricatures. Perhaps it was the age-old truth: if there is one thing worse than being talked about, it is *not* being talked about. Gillray was an escape valve, and thanks to him the public could laugh at the stupidity of their leaders. Gillray helped us discover that we did not need to guillotine our rulers – we could cut them down to size just by laughing at them.

There were of course others – from the gentle Henry Bunbury to the mischievous Richard Newton and the irrepressible Thomas Rowlandson. Father and son, Isaac and George Cruikshank, George Moutard Woodward and all the other caricaturists, helped establish a tradition of visceral political satire which still resonates to this day.

James Gillray was born in Chelsea on 13 August 1756, the middle of five children born to James, a Scottish soldier, and his wife Jane. Father had lost an arm at the Battle of Fontenoy in 1745, during the War of the Austrian Succession and had then become a sexton in the Moravian church. The sect believed in the essential depravity of man, and reckoned that children should be isolated from the influence of corruption. The young James Gillray was therefore brought up in a strict environment and at the age of 5 was sent away to board at a Moravian School at Bedford. That school folded after a few years, and as a result the 8-year-old James returned to Chelsea to live with his parents. Within a very short time, all his siblings had died (none of them reaching their tenth birthday). It must have made for a joyless childhood for James, but he showed a talent for draughtsmanship and was rewarded by being apprenticed to a lettering engraver in Holborn. Here he learned the basics of engraving, while producing maps, stationery and printed ephemera. In 1778 he was enrolled at the Royal Academy School, where he was a contemporary of William Blake. Together they must have made a formidable challenge to the teaching skills of Sir Joshua Reynolds and the Italian engraver Francesco Bartolozzi. Reynolds, always plugging away about painting in the grand manner and advocating conformity, must have been horrified at a pupil who paid his way through college by selling scurrilous and satirical etchings. He also gained paid employment as a book illustrator, providing engravings for Henry Fielding's *Tom Jones* and Oliver Goldsmith's *The Deserted Village*. From 1783 he spent three years trying to make a living producing true-to-life engravings – but by 1786 had returned to straight caricature.

Up until then, caricatures were often esoteric in nature – aimed at the people who already knew the subject being ridiculed. What marked Gillray out was his willingness to mock not just the monarchy, but the king as a person. He also, with others, developed the concept of John Bull as representing the British Public. He was especially vituperative in his depiction of the Tory Prime Minister, William Pitt, showing him as a pipe-cleaner figure, lining his own pocket and fleecing the taxpayer in frequently scatological situations. He was equally vicious in his portrayal of the other political giants of the age – the easily caricatured Charles James Fox with his louche lifestyle and permanent six o'clock shadow, the actor (and MP) Richard Brinsley Sheridan (always shown as a drunken sot, egging on others such as the Prince of Wales) and the Whig orator Edmund Burke. Gillray was living through tumultuous times – the loss of the American colonies, war with Napoleon, the illness of George III, and all of these events were meat and drink to a man such as Gillray.

To begin with, Gillray supplied his caricatures to a number of printshop owners, starting with William Holland and then Samuel William Fores. However, in 1791 he started an exclusive arrangement whereby his prints were sold by Hannah Humphrey. She was twenty years older than Gillray and there must have been raised eyebrows when he moved in with her at her premises above the printshop at 18 Old Bond Street. Together, they moved to 27 St James's Street, Piccadilly, in 1798.

The early 1800s saw a change in the target for Gillray's vitriol, with the one constant being his attack on the French. His print of *The Plumb Pudding in Danger*, showing William Pitt and the Emperor Napoleon sitting down at the dining table while carving up the globe of the world as if it were a plum pudding, came out in 1805. It is shown in Plate 5 and remains one of the most copied engravings of all time, dusted off and parodied on every occasion when Britain is at odds with its continental neighbours.

The world was changing: the odd couple of Pitt and Fox, political rivals but united by the pen of Gillray on so many occasions, both died in 1806. Sheridan failed to get re-elected in 1812. The old targets had gone, leaving Gillray to concentrate his merciless efforts on the French in general and Napoleon in particular. He also ensured that the royal family – especially the adulterous Prince of Wales and his brother the Duke of Clarence – were always being pilloried for their foibles and peccadilloes.

Not all of his output was political satire – he also published a large number of gentle and humorous prints, about the weather, about human frailties, about illness and medicine, and about fashions. In all, these accounted for perhaps a third of his lifetime's output of around a thousand engravings.

In time, Gillray proposed marriage to Hannah, reportedly getting as far as reaching the door to the church at St James's before turning away, with the words: 'This is a foolish affair, methinks, Miss Humphrey. We live very comfortably together; we had better let well alone.' Their commercial partnership remained firm – he needed her to sell his prints, and she needed him to supply the engravings. However, over time their personal relationship changed to the point that she was not just his housekeeper and companion, she became his nurse as, slowly and surely, he descended into mental instability and eventual insanity.

His eyesight had started to fail in 1807, meaning he could no longer see to work properly. A complete mental breakdown followed, and in 1811 he tried to commit suicide by hurling himself from a garret window – apparently unaware that it was secured with metal bars at the time. He took to wandering around the shop, naked and unshaven, and was last seen in that state on 1 June 1815. He died later that day and was buried in St James's Churchyard in Piccadilly six days later. Hannah survived him by just three years.

Gillray's fine draughtsmanship, his wit and his willingness to tackle topics which others fought shy of, single him out as a pioneer. He was at the vanguard of the Golden Age of Satire, and did as much to lead a revolution, a change in the way society worked and saw itself, as any of the industrialists of the period. In Britain we value freedom of speech – and never was that more demonstrated than in the caricatures of a man who rarely came out into the open. He was famous, both in England and on the continent, but he led a quiet and unassuming life away from public scrutiny. In terms of Art (with a capital A) he was perhaps the lowest of the low, described by a contemporary as 'a caterpillar on the green leaf of reputation'. But in terms of popular appeal, in terms of letting the public know what was going on in the corridors of power, in terms of producing images which had mass appeal and were collected by all groups across the whole spectrum of society, he had no equal.

Thomas Lawrence, 1769–1830

At first sight the inclusion of Thomas Lawrence, knight of the realm, painter in ordinary to His Majesty King George III, and a President of the Royal Academy, may seem somewhat incongruous. But his inclusion is justified just in order to show that the spotlight of fame can be turned off as well as on – Lawrence enjoyed fame in his lifetime but fell out of favour during the Victorian era, largely as a result of his perceived immoral lifestyle. Nowadays, we have come to expect that our painters lead a bohemian lifestyle – to drink, experiment with drugs, fornicate and generally set a bad example. It is seen, no doubt, as being part of the artist 'exploring the inner self'. But Lawrence had the misfortune to be followed almost immediately by the moralising Victorians, who tut-tutted at his indiscretions, and deemed him unsuitable and unworthy of praise. So the spotlight was turned off, and this magnificent artist has never quite regained his place alongside the British Greats of the world of painting.

It was not always thus; after Gainsborough died in 1788 and Reynolds died in 1792 Lawrence seemed to have taken over their mantle (although many would argue that he was a far finer portrait painter than Reynolds). He became *the* artist of his generation, the one commissioned to paint the portraits of all the movers and shakers of the Regency era, and all this from a man who was largely self-taught.

He was born in Bristol on 13 April 1769, one of only five out of sixteen children in the family to survive childhood. His father moved from Bristol to run the Black Bear Inn at Devizes, and the precocious young Thomas was already proving something of an artist and an entertainer. Father would apparently ask the tavern's customers: 'Which would you rather, young Tom recite a verse or paint your likeness?'

The tavern-keeping venture was a failure and his father was declared bankrupt. This left Thomas, then 10 years of age, as the family breadwinner. He moved to Bath, aged 11, and showed a considerable talent for portraiture, charging 3 guineas a sitting. He was entirely self-taught, using pastels at first then graduating to oils. His reputation soon spread and, still in his teens, he moved to London and installed his parents in a house in Greek Street and opened a studio at 41 Jermyn Street. Not bad for an 18-year-old!

He enrolled as a student at the Royal Academy but that sojourn did not last long – portrait painting was his only real interest. Over the ensuing thirty years he became the pre-eminent artist of his generation. His portraits of Nelson, Wellington and George IV are iconic representations of some of the great figures of Regency England.

With Lawrence it seems that it was not so much a case of falling in love, as falling in love too often; famously with two of the daughters of the actress Sarah Siddons at much the same time. He alternated between the two sisters, Sally and Maria, and on different occasions proposed marriage to both. The affairs caused enormous hurt to the family and at one stage this led him to have a complete nervous breakdown. In all likelihood Sarah Siddons herself held a torch for the charming artist, and certainly Lawrence seemed enraptured by her too, painting her portrait on at least fourteen occasions. The rumours got so bad that in 1804, Mr Siddons felt compelled to take out an advertisement in the newspapers of the day, expressly denying that his wife was having an affair with Lawrence. It is perhaps odd that the denial came from Mr Siddons, rather than from his wife – or indeed from Lawrence himself. Some years later, Lawrence was to fall head-over-heels in love with Sarah's niece, Fanny Kemble, a girl who, more than any other, closely resembled Sarah Siddons in her youth.

Some of the pain and anguish, and burning sadness, appears in the portraits he painted. By and large he seemed to excel at painting beautiful people, male or female. He knew how to bring out the best in good-looking sitters. However, he was hopeless at finishing projects – on one occasion taking twelve years to complete a commission; on his death, his studio was found to be littered with unfinished paintings, started and then abandoned.

Lawrence had a fairly alarming habit – at least, alarming for young and impressionable female sitters – of starting a commission by invading their personal space, coming right up alongside them and, from a distance of just a few inches, sketching a specific detail such as the nose or eyes. It must have been unnerving for anyone not used to feeling on their neck the warm breath of an adult male. No wonder half the female sitters look as though they have something very specific on their minds...

Over the years he painted portraits of royalty, including one in 1769 of Queen Charlotte. She hated it so much she refused to accept delivery of it and it remained in his studio until he died. Why didn't she like it? Probably because it captured something of the sadness of the woman behind the royal mask – and maybe she just didn't like being shown as a sort of 'Snow Queen', locked away inside her palace.

In time Lawrence was admitted to the Royal Academy, and in 1820 was made President of that august body. He had previously been appointed 'painter-in-ordinary' to George III, was knighted in 1814, and travelled through Europe at the request of the Prince Regent, painting foreign leaders such as Napoleon II, the Pope, the Tsar of Russia and miscellaneous archdukes, kings and emperors.

At the time of his death, Lawrence appears to have been at the height of his powers (but was nevertheless heavily in debt). He died on 7 January 1830 and almost immediately seems to have been airbrushed from history. Perhaps it was the Victorian reaction to the excesses and immorality of the Regency era, but the fact remains that from a height of popularity which far exceeded Constable and Turner, he then slumped into relative obscurity. Today, we may know his paintings, but we rarely see his name.

Lawrence was buried two weeks after his death, in the crypt at St Paul's Cathedral. The artist Turner was one of the mourners, and he later sketched the funeral from memory. Almost immediately there was a reaction against Thomas and his legacy. He went out of fashion, and the repugnance felt by society over his behaviour towards Sarah Siddons and her daughters was reignited in 1904 when his personal letters were published. The correspondence shows a highly emotional side to Lawrence, and he writes of his uncontrollable feelings and his anguish, while Mrs Siddons talks of 'this wretched madman's frenzy', and of his 'flying off in ANOTHER whirlwind'.

It took until the twentieth century for his reputation as a superb portrait painter to be restored; it was not before time.

John Joseph Merlin, 1735–1803

When the *Gentleman's Magazine* published an obituary of John Joseph Merlin in 1803, it described him as having lived at Princes Street, Hanover Square, and stated that he was a 'maker of Rose's Engines', as well as mathematical instruments, and that he was a 'watch and clock maker in general'. That description only told half the story.

Merlin was born near Huy in Belgium and was baptised in September 1735. It is likely that he came from a family of clockmakers, and he must have been something of a prodigy because at the age of 19 he went to Paris to study at the prestigious Academie des Sciences, where he learned about making watches and clocks for five years.

In this period, much emphasis for clockmakers was on inventing a device which could keep time so accurately that it could be used to calculate longitude on board long journeys at sea. There was a race between France, Britain, Spain and the Dutch to see who could come up with a solution. In England in 1759, John Harrison had just produced his revolutionary chronometer known as 'H4' – a watch which would prove to be a game-changer – and everybody in the trade would have wanted to see it. In 1760 the young Merlin got the chance to come to London as part of the entourage of the Conde de Fuentes, who had been appointed as the Spanish Ambassador to the Court of St James. He never went home.

If he had hoped to be able to gain admission to John Harrison's workshop, he would have been out of luck; Harrison expressly turned away a delegation of French watchmakers because at that stage, the watch was untested and had yet to gain approval from the Board of Longitude. But Merlin quickly found an outlet for his talents. Although it is unlikely that he spoke English when he first arrived, by 1763 he had left the service of Fuentes and had got a job in New Street Covent Garden, probably working for a goldsmith called Sutton. He would undoubtedly have met a jeweller-come-showman called James Cox, who specialised in gigantic and ornately decorated automata and clockwork instruments, and who had started a rather exclusive private museum in New Spring Gardens, near Admiralty Arch. When the museum opened officially in February 1772, Merlin was appointed 'the first or principal mechanic' to James Cox. The latter designed the ornate displays, with a huge raised gold dais surmounted by Zoffany's portraits of King George III and his wife Charlotte. Incorporated in the display was a concealed mechanical organ, which patriotically played *God Save the King* as the visitors completed their tour. Leading off from this reception area were a series of rooms filled with exotic automata, richly decorated with jewels.

The exhibits, such as a life-sized tiger in solid silver studded with precious stones, could move their heads from side to side – and that was where Merlin came in. His job was to design the machinery to imitate the movement of a wild animal – and in some cases that meant a whole series of machines, each controlling a different movement, and all inter-connected with a series of cams. One such exhibit still remains – the silver swan in the Bowes Museum at Barnard Castle – a testament to the extraordinary skills of a young mechanic who, for good measure, threw in a musical accompaniment to the graceful motion of the swan as it turns its head from side to side – and then lowers its head to produce a silver fish in its beak. One has to say that Merlin was a better machine-maker than a naturalist, since swans are vegetarian and do not eat fish....

Merlin was not, of course, the first person to experiment with automata, but the swan's complexity is astonishing: it has some 2,000 moving parts, including 139 crystal rods, and 113 rings in the neck alone. But this was no clumsy piece of jerky machinery housed inside an approximation of a bird; this was a silky-smooth elegant representation of nature – and it caused a sensation. Mark Twain viewing the swan when it was on display in Paris almost a century later remarked:

I watched the Silver Swan, which had a living grace about his movement and a living intelligence in his eyes – watched him swimming about as comfortably and

unconcernedly as if he had been born in a morass instead of a jeweller's shop –
watched him seize a silver fish from under the water and hold up his head and go
through the customary and elaborate motions of swallowing it...

The swan, and other automata like it, seemed to demonstrate that, in this enlightened age, man could imitate nature, could copy and improve upon it. The horizons appeared endless – and to that extent heralded the whole science of robotics and artificial intelligence.

Cox's problem was that he got the finances wrong; his hyper-expensive exhibits were affordable only to the imperial courts of Russia and China, or to the Moghul rulers in India. Charging viewers an entry fee of half a guinea per person – and then another half a guinea for a copy of the catalogue – was never going to work. Merlin left Cox's employment, determined to open his own museum of inventions in due course – and James Cox went bankrupt and had to try and sell all his exhibits by public lottery. It failed, and presumably most of the exhibits were scrapped and melted down for re-use.

It does not look as though Merlin had been employed by Cox on an exclusive basis – either that or, as the obituary notice in the *Gentleman's Magazine* made clear, Merlin was never idle and was always working on other projects in his spare time. In particular, he was making incredibly sophisticated machines for use by other workers in the jewellery trade – the Roses Machine mentioned in the obituary was a type of intricate lathe for engraving watch cases and so on. He also made a highly intricate and precise fusée engine – to cut the grooves in the fusées needed in contemporary watch mechanisms. On the other hand, Merlin also developed his own set of weighing scales – so that everyone could weigh themselves in the privacy of their own home. He was not necessarily the inventor of the concept of the 'Sanctorious Balance' (named after one Sanctorio Sanctorio, an Italian physician who had been born 200 years earlier). The user stood on the wooden platform and jotted down the recorded weight on a slate tablet set into the mahogany frame – while a bar could be raised or lowered to record height. This may have come from an idea Merlin had seen in France, but he saw the practical use of it and improved the design of the scales to make it more marketable.

Other highly practical inventions followed – not least the Dutch Oven. This was used to roast meat, using both the direct heat from the fire and the radiated heat from the cast iron casing. It incorporated an automatic baster and a spring-jack for turning the meat – an illustration of the way that Merlin was motivated by reducing the workload of servants. This was reflected in what was perhaps his most useful invention – a device which not just summonsed the servant when needed by his or her master – but informed them at the same time what was required, thereby saving a journey. The German writer Sophie von La Roche, writing about her visit to Merlin's emporium during her trip to London in 1786 describes it as follows:

> *I next came upon ... an invention whereby the servants should know immediately the bell rang in their master's room what was required, by means of a list fastened to the latter's bell, similar to a barometer, registering the orders which so constantly recur – water, broth, coffee, chocolate and the like. Now, since whoever pulls the bell simultaneously moves the pencil connected with the list in the servant's room, so this, the sound of the small bell, announces the employer's request to the servants – all of which is a great saving for the staff and results in rapid service, as English kitchens are in the basement with the servants' quarters.*

Another labour-saving device – though not perhaps one having such an obvious benefit – was a gadget enabling a hostess to dispense cups of tea to up to twelve guests without having to lift the cup to the tea pot on each occasion. By laying the twelve cups out on the device beforehand, the hostess could move each one into place beneath the steaming samovar by depressing a foot pedal. All she had to do was tap away with her foot, open the valve on the samovar, and voilà – tea is poured by the dozen!

Merlin took a particular interest in gadgets which could be of use to the disabled, and the most famous of these is the 'Gouty chair'. Once more, he probably did not invent this – but he certainly adapted it to become a highly popular way of aiding gout victims, and indeed of anyone too infirm to walk. Instead of being confined to bed, sufferers could be moved around on what was basically a chair mounted on three brass wheels. The patient could move the wheels by turning one or both of the brass winches situated by the arm rests. The legs of the patient could also be raised or lowered to a more comfortable position – in short it was an early form of wheelchair which brought comfort to tens of thousands of disabled people – including the unfortunate gout sufferers who were paying the price of a far-too-rich diet. Even the invalid King George III had the benefit of a Gouty Chair, with Dodsley's Annual Register for 1820 noting that, 'one of Merlin's chairs was at this time provided for him, with which he was so pleased, that he was constantly removed from one room to another in it.' The chairs often feature in Thomas Rowlandson's drawings (see Plate 3).

The Gouty Chair was merely one of a number of inventions designed to help the disabled. Another was a mechanical hand intended to help anyone who had lost a hand, enabling them to grip items. A machine to enable the blind to play whist was another – as was a device to help the infirm in and out of their carriages. Merlin developed a carriage for himself which included a 'waymaster' – the earliest form of measuring device showing the distance travelled. Another feature of the carriage was that the operator could manipulate the reins from inside the carriage, fully protected from inclement weather.

Another invention – or rather, a modification of an existing invention – was the hand-held scales for weighing gold coins. Its importance is a reflection on the problems of the gold currency in circulation at the time. Often coins were clipped, i.e., made smaller by virtue of the edges having been trimmed. Sometimes counterfeits were used, often with a high proportion of brass or other alloys. Coins could be rubbed smooth through use – in each case leaving the holder of the coin vulnerable to the bank refusing to exchange the coin for its full face value. Against this background, Merlin's handy pocket scales, using a steelyard and a micrometer screw, meant that the user could very accurately check the exact size and weight of any gold coin, from the guinea down to the quarter guinea. There were even equivalents designed for European currencies – a must-have for the travelling gentleman.

No one could accuse Merlin of being a one-trick pony. He also made amazingly complicated watches and clocks, some of which are in the Royal Collection. These included his own version of a perpetual motion clock – in other words, one which never required manual winding. It worked on changes in atmospheric pressure caused by temperature fluctuations.

Merlin made a host of delicate scientific instruments, but he was also capable of being quite frivolous, as with the 'invention' he is perhaps most famous for, the in-line skate. In practice these had been in use in Holland for over a century, and there is even a mention of one being used by an actor to glide effortlessly on stage during a performance of a play at Drury Lane Theatre in 1743. Nevertheless, Merlin came up with his own version, with three wheels of an identical size and positioned inline under a wooden rest, on which the foot was placed. The mistake Merlin made was to have the same size of wheel – had he had a smaller one at the front it would have enabled him to tilt forward and to use it as a brake. Instead, when he tried to create a sensation by gliding effortlessly in front of a startled audience at a swanky soiree, while playing the violin, it ended in disaster. Thomas Busby, writing in 1805 (some years after Merlin's death) explained the unfortunate incident:

One of his ingenious novelties was a pair of skaites contrived to run on wheels. Supplied with these and a violin, he mixed in the motley group of one of Mrs Cornely's masquerades at Carlisle House, Soho-Square; when not having provided the means of retarding his velocity, or commanding its direction, he impelled himself against a mirror of more than five hundred pounds value, dashed it to atoms, broke his instrument to pieces and wounded himself most severely.

The anecdote illustrates the high value of mirror glass, and also Merlin's love of playing music – as well as his wicked sense of humour. He loved playing tricks, and of being the centre of attention. He certainly played up to the image of an eccentric Belgian – a man who enjoyed the attention he received and the enjoyment he gave by 'dropping his haitches, strangling his vowels, and speaking in English but with very literal translations of French idioms and expressions'. Certainly this amused Fanny Burney, the diarist, who wrote in her diary in 1775 that:

> *He is a great favourite in our house ... very diverting also in conversation. There is a singular simplicity in his manners. He speaks his opinion on all subjects and about all persons with most undisguised freedom. He does not, though a foreigner, want words, but he arranges and pronounces them very comically.*

On another occasion she described him as 'Mr Merlin, the very ingenious mechanic.' Perhaps in time Fanny grew tired of his eccentricities and foibles – in later diary entries she called him 'that ridiculous Merlin', and described his 'inconceivable absurdities'.

Nevertheless, for some years he was part of the social circle which surrounded Fanny Burney and her father, the musicologist Dr Charles Burney. The circle included Dr Samuel Johnson, Thomas Gainsborough (who painted Merlin's portrait shown as Plate 2) and Hester Thrale. He rubbed shoulders with that inveterate gossip-monger Horace Walpole, and watched as Johann Christian Bach (son of Johann Sebastian Bach and generally known as John Bach, or even 'London Bach') played his newly designed harpsichords and pianos. It made for one of the most glittering intellectual and artistic gatherings of the period, and shows that Merlin was far more than a maker of toys and gadgets, or the man who tuned the pianos of the hosts and hostesses. For that is exactly what he did for customers who bought his musical instruments.

The design and manufacture of harpsichords, pianos – and hybrids of the two – appear to have dominated Merlin's time in the period up until around 1780, but after that time he seems to have concentrated more on his toys and automata. He had been involved in designing a barrel organ, intended for the mother of King George III, shortly after he arrived in England. This led on to a miscellany of strange and unusual instruments. Sophie von La Roche describes how these were shown to her when she visited Merlin:

> *During the afternoon we were taken to the mechanic and musician Merlin, to see and hear his pretty, but curious inventions: for he has tuned a grand-piano to sound*

as if all the instruments were invisibly emerging from it. The work and labour expended on this achievement call for respect, although I should consider myself unfortunate if I had to listen to it daily!

At the suggestion of Dr Charles Burney, Merlin came up with an instrument which increased the range of the piano so that it extended to six octaves, and another one which combined the square piano with an organ (making the square claviorganum). He also designed curiosities such as the five-string 'pentachord' (a variant on the four-string cello), and also devised special ratchet 'keys' to prevent strings losing tension.

In 1783 he acquired premises at 11 Princes Street, off Hanover Square (just South of Oxford Street), and he called the place Merlin's Mechanical Museum. Here he offered refreshments to visitors, with an advertisement stating that 'Ladies and Gentlemen who honour Mr Merlin with their Company may be accommodated with TEA and COFFEE at one Shilling each.' It cost 2*s* 6*d* to go in during the morning session (11 until 3) and 3*s* per evening session (7 until 9).

What they saw was an impressive array of automata and various inventions made by Merlin: 'At Merlin's you meet with delight', ran a contemporary ballad. In practice there was a whole cornucopia of delights, with the catalogue describing:

1. *Quartetto Music Cabinet*
2. *'Morpheus' and Gouty Chairs*
3. *The Library Table*
4. *The Tea Table*
5. *Sanctorius Balance*
6. *Large double Escarpolette, or swing*
7. *The Fire Screen*
8. *Valetudinarian Bedstead*
9. *Hygean Air Pump*
10. *A Curious Music Stand*
11. *The Hygeian Chair*
12. *The Prophetic Bell*

Many of these items were pieces of furniture adapted for multiple use. Sophie von La Roche recalls seeing:

Neat little writing- reading- or working-tables, combined with charming, soft-toned pianos ... others with pianos concealed, and clever desks with lights attached for quartettes, set up in less than three minutes, which, if not required for music, might be converted into a nice piece of furniture for playing chess.

Sophie went on to explain that Merlin was working on a room,

> *where Apollo is to sit enthroned, play his lyre and make a gesture meanwhile, by which a complete melody will be heard, though no instrument is visible. Apollo plays the gently melting Adagio of the piece alone upon the lyre, without accompaniment from the other instruments and machines, which appear dressed as waiters, and waitresses, and bring in any refreshments requested; thirty people can be present at a time and each performance is long enough for them to either breakfast or lunch. He hopes by the coming Spring to have everything ready for presentation....*

The 'large double Escarpolette, or swing', appears to have been a precursor of devices popular in parks and fairgrounds in later years. There is a record of a Merlin Swing having been constructed at Bath's Sydney Gardens and it is believed to have featured a boat-like contraption inside which two people could sit, as it swung up and down, accompanied by gentle music. Another variant was a precursor to the modern carousel, described as being an 'Aerial Cavalcade', and consisting of four wooden horses on a structure supported by six pillars, 'on which the Ladies and Gentlemen may ride, perfectly safe, over the heads of the rest of the company'. The cavalcade swept the paying public around in a circle while a hidden mechanical organ delighted the ear....

Interestingly, the catalogues were clearly aimed at the nobility and gentry, and also to 'all artists of genius'. The display combined an extraordinary mixture of both the frivolous and the practical – and if the contraptions and gadgets seem low-tech and even devoid of usefulness, think instead how they must have appeared to people seeing them for the first time. Here were labour-saving devices and gadgets which promised amusement in leisure time; they could see a brighter future beckoning, a future where machines could both take the strain and help entertain.

Merlin was not unique in the sense that others produced their own displays of automata and ingenious gadgetry, but he was an inspirational figure, and perhaps that is why he most deserves recognition. In one of his later catalogues for his Mechanical Museum, issued just before his death, he issued an invitation to 'young Amateurs of Mechanism'. One such youngster turned out to be the 8-year-old Charles Babbage, up on a visit to London from his home in Devon in around 1800. Merlin took the boy behind the scenes to see some of the items not on regular display, including two female figures around 12in high. One was an automaton which the boy later described as being 'singularly graceful', made of brass and clockwork, 'so as to perform almost every motion and inclination of the human body, viz. the head, the breasts, the neck, the arms, the legs etc.

even to the motion of the eyelids, and the lifting up of the hands and fingers to the face'. Babbage recalled that 'she used an eye-glass occasionally and bowed frequently as if recognizing her acquaintances'. But it was the second figure which captured the boy's imagination: she was 'an admirable danseuse, with a bird on the forefinger of her right hand, which wagged its tail, flapped its wings and opened its beak'. Babbage was completely captivated. 'The lady attitudinized in a most fascinating manner. Her eyes were full of imagination, and irresistible'.

What Merlin had done was demonstrate to an impressionable young boy that it was possible to programme a machine to perform a seemingly endless variety of movements. That lesson inspired Babbage through his later work on computers – his Analytical Machine and his Difference Engine.

Merlin died in 1803, and much of the stock owned by him at his museum was acquired by a rival called Thomas Weeks who had recently opened his own museum near the Haymarket. The danseuse was one of the items sold to Weeks, but visitors to his emporium were unable to see her even if they paid their half-a-crown admission – because she was left to languish in an attic. There she stayed until Weeks died in 1834. By then Babbage was an engineer and an entrepreneur in his own right, and he was also the heir to a fortune built up by his father, a wealthy banker. Somehow he found time to attend the auction of the items in the estate of Thomas Weeks – and for £35 was able to buy the figure of the dancer.

Thereafter she was placed on display on a glass pedestal in the drawing room next to where Babbage's unfinished Difference Engine was being displayed to visitors. Babbage liked to note that his more frivolous guests – invariably the ones from Britain – were far more interested in the beguiling dancer than they were with the half-finished computer. Only the foreigners, who were invariably more serious-minded, seemed to appreciate the attraction of the calculating engine over the 'fascinating and graceful movements' of the dancer.

Before exhibiting her, Babbage had disassembled the dancer and checked all the parts. He was amazed to see that the interior was riddled with trial holes, suggesting that rather than being designed in accordance with detailed plans, a lot of Merlin's work started off intuitively, and was then followed up by hours and hours of trial and error until 'perfection' was achieved. Merlin indeed deserved the accolade in the *Gentleman's Magazine* that he was:

an ingenious mechanic, as has been long known to the publick; his good qualities as a man will be long remembered by those who knew him. Of an active disposition, he scarcely let a single moment slip by unemployed, notwithstanding his health had been long on the decline.

He died in London on 4 May 1803, and apart from bequests to servants and to the young daughter of the owner of the stables where he kept his horse, he left his property to his two brothers and a sister. Unwilling to see his beloved horse ridden by anyone else, he left express instructions that the animal, then aged 30, was to be put down. Two centuries later, and Merlin is just a footnote in history. He was a genius who deserves to be better remembered.

James 'Athenian' Stuart, 1713–1788

For an era in British history which is renowned for its architecture, it is surprising how few notable architects there were. History especially remembers William Kent, John Soane, James Wyatt, the John Woods (father and son) and William Chambers, founder-member of the Royal Academy. If it is narrowed down to neoclassical styles, the list generally consists of one name: Robert Adam, although he was aided by his brothers John and James. That is somewhat unfair on a number of others who contributed to the neoclassical movement, none more so than James 'Athenian' Stuart.

Stuart was not from an artistic background; his father was a Scottish sailor living in London's Ludgate Street at the time of James's birth in 1713. The family was reduced to total poverty when his father died, leaving James the eldest of three siblings. As a young boy he showed artistic talent, and was sent to learn the trade as a fan-painter in the employment of Lewis Goupy. His employer was a French miniaturist and portrait painter living in Covent Garden, and no doubt encouraged the young lad to learn foreign languages – including Latin, Italian and Greek. Whatever money he earned had to go to support his mother and younger brother and sister; after his mother died, however, he decided to pack in his job and travel to Italy. Not for him the luxury of a coach in which to carry out a Grand Tour – for James it meant travelling on foot.

He started his continental wanderings in 1742 at the age of 29, arriving in Italy where he took employment as a guide, or *cicerone*, showing antiquities to visiting members of the aristocracy. He also polished up his language skills and improved his talents as an artist, with a particular interest in producing studies of buildings. After nine years he then journeyed to Greece with his friend (and later biographer) Nicholas Revett, intent on carrying out the first methodical study of ancient classical Greek remains.

The expedition was sponsored, in part, by the Society of Dilettanti. This had been founded in 1734 as a society of aristocrats and scholars intent on studying classical art. Up until then, Greek and Roman styles were lumped together as 'classical', whereas Stuart and Revett, with their meticulous measurements and drawings, helped show that there was a distinct Greek style. Both the Romans and the Greeks had used Ionic and Doric columns – although the Romans tended to favour the more elaborately-topped Corinthian columns – but more significantly the Greeks tended to use post-and-lintel door frames, whereas the Romans used arches. Furthermore, the Roman mastery of using concrete enabled them to make more complicated shapes – such as the domed arch of the Pantheon, whereas Greek architecture was simpler and less cluttered. In identifying these differences and by producing accurate measurements and drawings, the work of Stuart and Revett helped launch the neoclassical movement. A Greek revival swept through Britain and Europe in the latter part of the Georgian era. The catalyst was his seminal work *Antiquities of Athens*, published in four volumes over the period between 1762 and 1816. This monumental work set a new benchmark in accurate archaeological recording. It included hundreds of images of buildings, plans, sculpture, friezes, and decorative objects such as vases. Suddenly, aficionados of all-things-Greek could study the treasures of Ancient Greece from the comfort of their own homes, without having to travel.

Stuart had returned to Britain in 1755 to start work on the first volume of *Antiquities of Athens*. It only dealt with five buildings in the north of Athens and the publication of just this one volume involved Stuart in years of dedicated and scholarly work, preparing the engravings, designing the neoclassical binding, proofing and so on. The result was a masterpiece which was to become the go-to reference work for all subsequent architects, interior designers and antiquarians with an interest in the Greek Revival movement. Its significance spread throughout Europe and across the Atlantic – even Thomas Jefferson, President of the United States between 1801 and 1809, owned a copy of the first volume. Subsequent volumes were published posthumously, in 1790, by his widow Elizabeth and with third and fourth volumes coming out in 1795 being based upon his drawings and descriptions.

By the Regency period the Greek Revival movement was in full swing, with buildings such as the Theatre Royal at Covent Garden (1808–09), the General Post Office (1824–29) the British Museum (1823–48), the Wilkins Building at University College, London (1826–30) and the National Gallery (1832–38). Elsewhere, Edinburgh sported so many buildings adorned with Doric columns and classical proportions that it was dubbed 'the Athens of the North'. Eventually of course, it was succeeded by the neo-Gothic style so beloved by the Victorians, but in its heyday – say, 1800 to 1837 – it became associated with a 'Greek mania' which swept the country, no doubt inspired in part by the appearance of the Elgin marbles at the British Museum after 1817. It was a movement affecting not just exteriors of buildings, but all the interior features, right down to the 'Greek key' designs on glassware, and the rediscovery of the tripod form, which led to furniture such as marble-topped sideboards mounted on three legs. At the same time, egg-and-dart decorations appeared on ceiling mouldings across the land.

Stuart's book became an invaluable sourcebook for generations of architects and interior designers. His own designs for metal work, his sculptures, his paintings all became a major influence. His scholarship was recognised by the Royal Society, who admitted him as a Fellow in 1758, with a citation which started with the words:

> *Mr James Stuart of Grosvenor Square History painter and Architect, eminent in his profession and who hath particularly applyed himself to the study of antiquity, during a long residence in Greece and Italy....*

Having obtained a reputation as a connoisseur and an authority on ancient Greece, he received a number of commissions to design country houses – and in particular, to extend and alter existing country homes. He was involved in the designs for garden cottages at Shugborough Hall (just on the edge of Cannock Chase in Staffordshire), along with some of the interiors. He is also associated with follies and garden buildings at Hagley Hall in Worcestershire. He designed the Temple of the Winds, an octagonal building at Mount Stewart in Northern Ireland, based upon the second-century BC clocktower known as The Tower of the Winds in Athens. Other works are represented in the interiors at Kedleston Hall in Derbyshire and at Belvedere in Bromley, Kent. The interior of the chapel in the Royal Naval Hospital in Greenwich owes much to Stuart after he was appointed Surveyor to the Hospital.

He was also instrumental in illustrating numerous books on classical designs, and he filled copious notebooks with designs for fireplaces, chimneys and wall decorations. In addition, he designed commemorative medals and plaques, including some which were then minted by Mathew Boulton.

Here was a man on the cusp of a great movement – and then he drifted away from the central scene, leaving it to others such as Robert Adam. Why the lack of a continuing push towards a Greek revival movement? Probably because he was no longer a driven man. Although it is not clear how he came into money, it seems that he no longer needed to work for a living. His time and energies were dissipated on eating and drinking and, oddly, playing skittles down at his local pub. He had long been notorious for being slow in completing commissions – now he was totally unreliable and frequently worse for wear through drink, which in turn exacerbated his recurring gout attacks.

One also gets the impression that he was not trying to launch a movement, so much as provide accuracy to a period of history he loved. Robert Adam publicly loathed Stuart's designs, but still went and used many of the features in his own architectural works. It was a time when the ever-expanding British Empire was coming into contact with different influences from all across the globe. Cook's voyages of the Pacific brought Oceania into vogue; trade with China and the Far East led to a fashion for chinoiserie in all manner of decorations; the early explorations in Egypt towards the end of the eighteenth century brought about a mania for Egyptian décor, while the discoveries at Herculaneum and Pompeii triggered a fascination with ancient Rome. Stuart's Greek revival became part of a neoclassical movement which dominated architecture for much of the following century, not so much in its 'pure' recreation of Stuart's vision of ancient Greece, but after absorbing many other influences.

The Grecian influence was felt right the way through to the clothes worn by women. If we think of what was fashionable in the 1780s, we think of heavy brocades, lots of lace and high, powdered wigs. But by 1800 tastes had changed – out went the stiffly formal garments and in came light muslin dresses, free flowing and revealing (as opposed to concealing) what lay beneath. Whether you call it 'Empire line' or 'Regency', it was all inspired by ancient Greece, and was thanks to the influence of men like James Stuart. In particular, the turn of the century saw the development of classical ornamentation using geometric shapes. These patterns were repeated over and over, typically with the Greek key motif. These geometric patterns were everywhere – on sleeves, on shawls and around hems; Greek-style strappy footwear was popular and hairstyles and accessories displayed their classical origins. Grecian styles were copied and developed but kept the basic theme of high waistlines, or with tunics made of pale-coloured fabrics clinging to the body. Materials were loosely draped, emulating styles on statues of Greek goddesses.

Little is known about Stuart's private life. He was reported to have married when in his younger days – to a woman variously described as his housekeeper and as 'a Grecian lady'. It is not known when or where she died, but at the age of 67, James Stuart again embarked on matrimony, this time with a servant girl called Elizabeth, who was then aged 20. She bore him five children, two of whom died in his lifetime. As for James, he died suddenly at his home in Leicester Square on 2 February 1788 and was buried in the crypt of St Martin-in-the-Fields. Robert Adam, whose works completely overshadowed those of James Stuart, died four years later, and hence neither of them lived to see the century in which their influences really bore fruit.

Drawing of the Temple of the Winds by James Athenian Stuart.

Chapter 8

Schemers, Dreamers – and a Pair of Potters

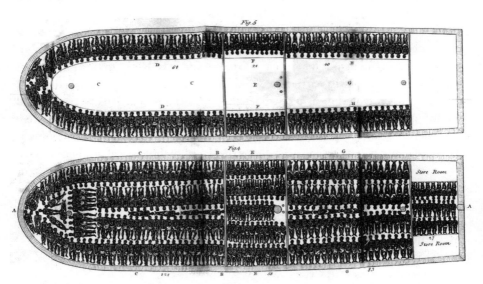

Diagram of the *Brookes*, showing the condition in which slaves were transported across the Atlantic. A copy diagram formed part of the visual aids displayed by Thomas Clarkson.

Thomas Clarkson 1760–1846

If people are asked to name the powerhouse behind the movement for the abolition of slavery, probably ninety-nine people out of a hundred would come up with the name of William Wilberforce. He was certainly the mouthpiece – or at least, the parliamentary mouthpiece – of the abolition movement. But he was definitely not the powerhouse of the drive to abolish the slave trade. A devout Christian, Wilberforce was always introspective and wracked by a lack of self-confidence, unsure of the best way to serve God, and needing regular reassurance and pressure from others to keep putting forward the anti-slavery cause in front of his fellow members of parliament. His friends, especially the so-called Testonites such as James Ramsay, Lady Middleton and Hannah More, often needed to cajole and coax him to stay with the job of steering legislation through parliament. They helped write his speeches and coached him on his presentation. And above all, one man made the bullets for Wilberforce to fire – and that man was Thomas Clarkson.

For over fifty years they worked together towards the eradication of the pernicious trade in human beings. Yet, after Wilberforce died in 1833, and his biography was written by his two sons Robert and Samuel as a five-volume set, Clarkson was virtually written out of the story. It must have been most hurtful to a man who had spent his entire adult life single-mindedly campaigning to end slavery, to find his contribution sidelined and dismissed as being peripheral. The embittered Clarkson came out of retirement to publish his side of the story in a tract called *Strictures on a Life of William Wilberforce* and the brothers were forced to issue a mealy-mouthed apology and to alter some of the text in subsequent editions. Even setting aside the fact that the sons were bound to want to put their father in a favourable light, it was a shameful episode, but it worked. The damage had been done and in the minds of the public it had been a one-man show - that of Wilberforce.

Clarkson was the true powerhouse, described by the poet Samuel Taylor Coleridge as a 'moral steam engine'. Throughout a period of sixty-one years he had devoted his life to the cause, and no one worked more tirelessly, or gave more of themselves than this extraordinary man.

He was born on 28 March 1760 in Wisbech in Cambridgeshire. His father, John, was an Anglican priest who worked as headmaster at the local grammar school. John died when Thomas was 6, but Thomas attended the grammar school until the age of 15, when he became a pupil of St Paul's School in London. As a 19-year-old he was admitted to St John's College, Cambridge to read mathematics and he graduated in 1783. He was then ordained as a priest, but never practised as a clergyman. Contemporaries at Cambridge described him as being somewhat humourless, a large, slightly ponderous and thoughtful man.

Above all, he was ambitious for success and, having won a university competition for an essay written in Latin in 1784, he decided to enter the competition the following year. The topic for the essay had been set as the question: 'Is it lawful to enslave the unconsenting?' It was not a subject Clarkson had ever considered, and as far as he was concerned it was merely 'an innocent contest for literary honour'. He did his research, composed his essay – and duly won the prize. And that was when his life changed forever.

It was a tradition that the winner would attend the Senate House at College and read the winning entry, and on his way back to London afterwards, Clarkson was apparently overcome with thinking about the whole subject of slavery. It was, he reasoned, not enough to write essays in Latin – someone had to do something to end the trade. Later, Clarkson describes his epiphany, when he realised that this was to be his life's work and that the 'someone' was going to be him. He apparently got out of his carriage, and sat on the ground while holding the reins of his horse, and realised that he had found his life's cause. It was at Wadesmill in Hertfordshire, at a spot now marked by a commemorative plaque.

With the support of a number of Quaker friends, Clarkson edited his essay, translated it into English and had it published in 1786 so that it could gain public acceptance. Clarkson read all the available information gathered about the slavery trade, and condensed it down into a pamphlet published in 1787 under the title of *A Summary View of the Slave Trade and of the Probable Consequences of Its Abolition.* The problem was that up until that time, the wider public had been largely unaware of the horrors of the slave trade – not that they approved or disapproved, more that they simply did not know what was involved. Clarkson saw it as his job to show people exactly what was involved. He travelled from town to town, city to city armed with the most powerful of visual aids – his Africa Box containing manacles, leg irons and head restraints. He handed round the powerful image of the *Brookes* slave ship showing the slaves in crowded rows, one after the other, filling every inch of the available space on board. And he contrasted this by showing other items – articles of decoration made by Africans, showing their skill and artistry. These were people; people with feelings, with talents; they should not be treated as animals.

The appeal to the public was on different levels; to some, Clarkson would demonstrate that the suffering was inhumane; to others he might arouse anger that the slavers were missing out on the opportunity to 'bring the native African to God'. With others – even the sailors who embarked on slaving voyages – he might appeal to the fact that the conditions on board during the middle passage – the trip from the west coast of Africa to the plantations in the Caribbean colonies – were so appalling that diseases such as typhus spread like wildfire. Such diseases killed perhaps 20 per cent of all on board, and the infection was no respecter of status, killing slave and sailor alike. Even the wealthy merchants could relate to the Clarkson proposition that the use of slaves simply did not make economic sense: taking the per-capita cost of buying the slaves, shipping them across the Atlantic, feeding them, and suffering the huge losses resulting from low life-expectancy, coupled with the declining returns and limited life of the Caribbean soils, meant that slavery was unsustainable.

Clarkson did not mind why people signed his petitions; all that mattered was that they signed. He knew no fear – he would go and campaign in pubs and taverns in cities such as Bristol, Liverpool and Manchester – cities whose prosperity was built on the slave trade in one way or another. On one occasion he was cornered by a gang of eight who had apparently been paid to throw him into the dock to drown, but he managed to knock over one of the assailants and escape with his life. In his words: 'I darted forward, one of them, against whom I pushed myself, fell down. Their ranks were broken and I escaped, not without blows, amid their imprecations and abuse.'

1787 saw the formation of the first committee for the abolition of the slave trade. It marked a huge step forward in the campaign. Up until that time the main anti-slavery proponents were Quakers. They suffered from two problems. The first is that they were perceived as figures of fun. Even the name 'Quaker' was intended as a way of ridiculing people who 'quaked' in the face of their Lord. If they were not taken seriously, the other drawback was even more significant: they could not be elected to parliament. As Dissenters they had no real voice, were not allowed to stand as an MP, and their influence was limited to 300 of their adherents presenting a petition to the Houses of Parliament in 1783. The Honourable Members and their Lordships took absolutely no notice. But the Quaker leaders, ever pragmatic, responded by broadening their appeal by siding with leading figures in the Anglican community who shared their views. Of the twelve members of the new committee, nine were Quakers, plus Thomas Clarkson and two other Anglicans. Wherever Clarkson pinned up a notice calling for a meeting to discuss the slave trade, he could rely on Quaker adherents to make sure that he had a supportive audience. He never actually became a member of the Society of Friends, but he clearly identified with many of the tenets of their faith, telling the Tsar of Russia in 1816 that he was 'nine parts in ten in their way of thinking'. Ten years earlier he had published a three-volume book called *A Portraiture of Quakerism*.

The new committee, known as The Society for Effecting the Abolition of the Slave Trade ('SEAST') was formed on 22 May 1787. It met with William Wilberforce and agreed that he should put forward a proposal that parliament should set up an inquiry to look into the slave trade. In doing so, the committee was sensible enough to realise that an outright attack on slavery itself was too ambitious a target, and that first of all they should campaign against the *trade* in slaves. Abolition of slavery itself could be phase two.

This was where Clarkson's petitions proved invaluable, as he criss-crossed the country, travelling thousands of miles year in and year out, stirring up public opinion, informing people and making sure that the issue was debated as a matter of concern to the whole nation. It is estimated that in the first seven years after SEAST was formed Clarkson rode over 35,000 miles, taking in all the major towns and cities. Anti-slave-trade groups were set up in his wake, adding to the swelling numbers calling for reform. Wilberforce, meanwhile, submitted his proposals for the abolition of the trade year after year, and on every such occasion parliament chucked the scheme out. MPs were simply protecting their own interests – they were, when all was said and done, the landowners and the wealthy merchants who stood most to gain from being able to run Caribbean plantations with cheap i.e. slave labour.

In 1791 parliament yet again inflicted a heavy defeat on the Wilberforce-backed Bill to halt the trade in slaves, voting 163 to 88 against the motion. It sparked off a protest, which Clarkson supported, namely a boycott of West Indian sugar.

Households up and down the country, in their hundreds and thousands, 'did their bit' by giving up sugar altogether, or opting for more expensive sugar from the East Indies, produced by free labour. It was a campaign which motivated not just the electorate – indeed it gave a voice to a huge swathe of people who could not vote, including, of course, women. They were the ones making the shopping decisions and, whipped up by some very effective marketing, their decision was to 'say no' to Caribbean 'slave sugar'. The boycott hit the interests of the wealthy merchants who traded in Caribbean sugar where it hurt most – in their pockets.

Up until that time the import of sugar had been astonishing. Take Liverpool for instance, which in 1704 imported just 760 tons of sugar – a century later the imports were a staggering 46,000 tons. Bristol had the same story, competing with Liverpool in the race to export textiles, small arms and gunpowder to Africa; trading goods for slaves to take from Africa to the West Indies; and then trading these for sugar and rum to take back to Britain from the Caribbean.

The campaign against slave sugar was boosted in 1791 when William Fox published an anti-sugar pamphlet. It ran to twenty-five editions and sold 70,000 copies. One paragraph should suffice to set the tone:

> *If we purchase the commodity we participate in the crime. The slave dealer, the slave holder, and the slave driver, are virtually agents of the consumer, and may be considered as employed and hired by him to procure the commodity…. In every pound of sugar used we may be considered as consuming two ounces of human flesh.*
> *William Fox, 1791, in Address to the People of Great Britain).*

The boycott spread rapidly until by 1794 it is estimated that well over 300,000 families had joined the protest. Grocers reported that demand had fallen by a third. The royal family were shown by Gillray as joining in the boycott (see Plate 5), with the numerous daughters of George III complaining at being asked to go without their sugar.

But the climate for change altered completely when war with France broke out: the abolition movement was seen as being damaging to national interests and SEAST recognised that now was not the time to rock the boat. Clarkson went into semi-retirement and in 1794 his friends, who included Wilberforce, raised £1,500 by way of compensation for his costs and expenses. The poor man was utterly exhausted and in weak health. 1794 saw him buy a small estate near Ullswater, where he became friends with the poet William Wordsworth. Two years later he married Catherine Buck, a girl from Bury St Edmunds in Suffolk. Together they had a child, born the same year, and in due course the family moved to Bury St Edmunds for the sake of Catherine's health.

It was not until 1804 that the abolitionists judged that it was time to renew their mission, and it meant that Clarkson yet again took to his saddle and rode around the country whipping up support. By now, the general public had got the message. It was also at a time when plantation owners were beginning to accept that higher production costs and diminishing yields linked to overworked soil on their plantations was making the high cost of transporting slaves uneconomic. Finally, in 1807, parliament passed the Slave Trade Act.

Clarkson next turned his attention to stopping the slave trade in other countries – in America, in France and in the rest of Europe. In 1808 he published *The History Of The Rise, Progress And Accomplishment Of The Abolition Of The Slave-Trade by the British Parliament*, and six years later went to Paris to try and promote a timetable for the abolition of the trade.

When what became known as the Anti-Slavery Society was formed in 1823, Clarkson once more hit the road, travelling 10,000 miles to promote the cause of emancipation, encouraging petitions (there were 777 of them delivered to parliament) and supporting local groups and anti-slavery societies. In 1833 the Slavery Abolition Act was finally passed. Clarkson went on to live a further thirteen years – during which time he continued to support the abolition cause, speaking at conferences, and supporting the work of the British and Foreign Anti-Slavery Society which was formed in 1840. In June that year the Society's convention elected Clarkson as their president and he was given a standing ovation by the 5,000 delegates who had gathered from all over the world.

Clarkson died on 26 September 1846 at his home in the tiny Suffolk village of Playford, at the age of 86. Unlike Wilberforce, who was buried in the north transept of Westminster Abbey after a funeral attended by all the great and the good, Clarkson was laid to rest in the small churchyard of the local church. Few from London and beyond made the journey to witness the internment. That says it all, really.

John Gill, 1697–1771

In the twenty-first century the importance of the Christian religion seems to be receding into the background, with declining church attendances. But in the eighteenth century, religious faith was the backbone of human endeavour across the board. The scientists, the industrialists, the movers and shakers of the industrial revolution were generally strong believers in the Divine. It was their faith which drove them on, made them challenge the existing order, required them to try and try again until new ways could be found to solve problems. And so, whereas it may appear odd to modern readers to include a theologian as a giant, in many ways it is entirely appropriate.

If history books of the period are anything to go by, it is to be assumed that the great religious thinkers and scholars of the age were brothers John and Charles Wesley and fellow cleric Charles Whitfield (together, founders of the Methodist movement). Yet there is one figure – in a period dominated by religious disputes and pamphleteering wars – who stands out as perhaps the most knowledgeable theologian of the eighteenth century, a man whose writings are still highly influential especially within the Baptist movement. His name is John Gill.

At the start of the eighteenth century, the majority of Dissenters were Presbyterians, followed by the Congregationalists (independents) and then by the Quakers and then the Baptists. Small in number, even by 1798 there were only 445 Baptist churches in England and Wales with 30,000 members. But the influence of the Baptist movement was considerable, especially in the New World, and Gill fostered and encouraged the growth of Baptist beliefs in America, not least by leaving many of his theological books to Rhode Island College, now Brown University. In his will he bequeathed a complete set of his works and many of his library books to that institution. Rhode Island was where the first Baptist church had been set up in the 1630s by Roger Williams, aimed at early settlers from England. Nowadays there are some 50 million Americans who claim to be Baptists, and the Baptist faith has been synonymous with America's startling growth over the past 200 years.

John Gill was born in November 1697 and died in 1771 – his life corresponded with a period where Dissenters flourished. This was in part because the 1689 Toleration Act granted Nonconformists the freedom to express themselves publicly, especially in print. It was an era in which the words of clergymen could command national attention, and it has been said that 'in an age in which young churches were looking to wise heads for guidance, John Gill was the principal wise head sought on matters of theological orthodoxy.' He became a towering figure in the Baptist movement, and there could have been few people with a deeper knowledge of the Bible, and in particular of the Old Testament.

Little could have been predicted for him when John Gill was born, the son of a poor woollen merchant in the Northamptonshire town of Kettering. His parents, Eric and Elizabeth, sent him to the local grammar school until he was 11 – and that marked the end of his formal education; from then on, he was self-taught in everything. He learned Latin, he learned Greek, he immersed himself in a copy of Buxtorf's Grammar and Lexicon and thereby taught himself Hebrew; he read classical literature; he studied logic and rhetoric – all without formal teaching assistance. That must have marked him out as a somewhat unusual young boy in his teens, and a short biography, written in 1838 by John Rippon, refers to the fact that the young Gill 'gained marks of distinction from several of the neighbouring clergy, who condescended, occasionally, to examine and encourage his progress, when they met him at a bookseller's shop in the town, which he constantly attended on market days....'

He was baptised on 1 November 1716 at the age of 19, and shortly afterwards began preaching. In 1718, he spent a few months among the Baptist congregation at Higham Ferrers, Northamptonshire. While there, he met and married Elizabeth Negus and the following year he and his new bride moved to London and joined the Baptist congregation at Goat Yard Chapel at Horsleydown, in Southwark. It was at Horsleydown that he was ordained on 22 March 1720, and he remained there as minister for an impressive fifty-one years. During that time the congregation outgrew the premises, and in 1758 it re-sited to Carter Lane in Southwark.

Gill's studies of the Scriptures, and especially of the originals written in Hebrew, brought him into contact with John Skepp, a fellow Baptist and one of the foremost Hebrew scholars of his era. Skepp had a particularly impressive collection of Hebrew and Rabbinical books. Unlike many of his contemporaries, Gill did not disrespect the Jewish theologians, recognising that, since the entire Old Testament was written by Jews, the only way to 'get into their heads' was to study Hebrew and read their books. His eventual successor, John Rippon, describes this unusually tolerant view with these words:

He plainly saw, that as the New Testament was written by men who had all of them been Jews, and who, notwithstanding their being inspired, must needs retain and use many of the idioms of their language, and allude to rites, ceremonies, and customs peculiar to that people; so the writings of the Jews, especially the more ancient ones, who lived nearest the times of the apostles, could not but be of use for the better understanding the phraseology of the New Testament, and the rites and customs to which it frequently alludes.

When Skepp died, Gill purchased much of his library and his fluency in Hebrew gave him access to an extraordinarily wide variety of theological works. In 1723 Gill began a series of sermons – 122 in all, on the Song of Solomon. This was to establish a pattern which would last throughout his ministry. His sermons did not make easy listening in the sense that he offered no easy options – he was a High Calvinist, vigorously orthodox on Christian basics, and he demanded the highest standard of commitment from his followers. In 1728 he published the underlying ideas behind his sermons in his *Exposition of the Book of Solomon's Song*. He then embarked on his magnum opus – a commentary on the entire Bible, a complete systematic theology published as his *Exposition of the Old and New Testaments*. This was the first time that this had ever been attempted: a verse-by-verse analysis of the entire

Bible. The New Testament commentary was published between 1746 and 1748 and ran to three volumes; the Old Testament commentaries ran to six volumes, finished by Gill in 1766, five years before he died.

Many Baptist ministers today still refer to this work, and to his *Body of Doctrinal and Practical Divinity* which was published in 1769. Recognised in his lifetime as a remarkable theologian, he was awarded a Doctorate of Divinity by Aberdeen University in 1748. The citation referred to his attainments as an 'extraordinary proficiency in sacred literature, the Oriental tongues, and Jewish antiquities.' His output of writings was enormous, earning him the sobriquet of 'Dr Voluminous'. Throughout his ministry he inspired audiences and caused many newcomers to 'give in their experience' and to become baptised.

Rippon refers to Gill as being 'of the middle stature, neither tall nor short, well proportioned, a little inclined to corpulency; his countenance was fresh and healthful, expressive of vigour of mind, and of a serene cheerfulness, which continued with him almost to the last.'

Gill had been living in Gracechurch Street, Camberwell, and died there in October 1771, or, as Rippon floridly remarked: 'Thus he gloriously terminated his mortal career, without a sigh or groan, on the 14th day of October 1771, at about eleven o'clock in the forenoon … aged seventy-three years, ten months, and ten days.' He was buried in the Dissenters burial ground at Bunhill Fields – the final resting place of men such as Daniel Defoe and William Blake.

Modern audiences may care little for the religious disputes which caused such division and heated arguments in the eighteenth century: debates about Anabaptists, hyper-Calvinism and predestination simply do not occupy our minds at the breakfast table. But it is worth remembering that 250 years ago these matters were discussed and debated furiously. And, as one modern website suggests: 'To say that Dr Gill influenced evangelical Christians in general and Baptists in particular is like saying the sun influences the daytime.'

One website which contains the entirety of Gill's commentary on the Old and New Testaments suggests: 'Most people today have never heard of John Gill. This is unfortunate, since his works contain priceless gems of information that are found nowhere except in the ancient writings of the Jews.' More significantly, he gave impetus to a form of evangelical Protestantism which took root in the United States, where it remains to this day. Dr Gill – you deserve your time under the spotlight, however much you would have hated and despised the idea of personal fame.

John Howard, 1726–1790

It is almost as if history can only cope with one do-gooder in a hundred-year period – and the Georgian era has William Wilberforce. As already meantioned, he was the parliamentary spokesman for the abolitionist movement and in later life devoted his energies to promoting animal welfare. No matter that he had a team of tireless workers operating in the background, encouraging him and giving him the backbone to see his mission through: he was a philanthropist and definitely a doer of good deeds. But he wasn't the only one, and history should also remember a man who worked almost alone in his tireless devotion to promoting the interests of one of the most unfashionable sections of the community – the prison population. His name lives on through the Howard League for Penal Reform, founded in 1866, nearly ninety years after the publication of his seminal work *The State of the Prisons*. But his is not a name which is generally well known, even if his contribution to changing the face of society has been considerable.

John Howard was born in 1726, probably in Hackney in London's East End. As with so many of the names featured in this book he was born into a family of Dissenters. As with many other Nonconformists, he would never have the chance of going to university or of joining the professions, but this very restriction gave him the ability to challenge the accepted order, 'to think outside the box', and to come up with ideas for change. Ironically, his parents' Nonconformist beliefs did not mean that he was given a particularly good education, unlike so many children from dissenting families. Indeed, Howard was acutely aware, throughout his life, that his schooling was so poor that he never really mastered the rules of grammar, spelling or punctuation. Instead he got seven years of lectures on hellfire and damnation from a strict Calvinist preacher called John Worsely. He then spent some time at an academy at Newington Green before becoming apprenticed to a firm of wholesale grocers.

John was a sickly child and suffered from ill health for much of his life. His mother died when he was an infant, and when his father died in 1742, John, then aged 16, inherited enough wealth to enable him to buy out his Articles of Apprenticeship. His father had been a partner in a business selling carpets and upholstered goods and owned a small estate at Cardington in Bedford. At that stage in his life, John was at a crossroads. He no longer had any parental guidance. He was wealthy and, like so many others, he could simply have gone off the rails and devoted his energies to drinking, whoring and gambling. The fact that he did not do any of these things is a testament to his religious convictions and a strong desire to help others. Initially he travelled to Europe, but poor health brought him back to Stoke Newington, where he was looked after by a landlady called Sarah. She was twice his age. They were married in 1752, but Sarah was also in poor health and died just three years later.

Events elsewhere in Europe prompted a new impetus to John Howard's life. On 1 November 1755, ten days before Sarah died, a huge earthquake had torn Lisbon apart. As mentioned in the profile of John Michell, the city was then ravaged by fire and a tsunami. Estimates vary, but tens of thousands of people are believed to have died. News of the tragedy reached London a few days later, but not until after enormous waves, caused by the tsunami, had reached the English coastline. The fact that the disaster had happened on All Saints Day made the catastrophe all the more appalling. Newly widowed and no doubt profoundly affected by his personal loss, Howard set off for Portugal by ship, only for the vessel to fall prey to a French privateer operating out of the French port of Brest. Howard was captured, thrown into a dungeon, and kept in conditions which were little short of inhuman. It was in all probability the first time Howard had ever seen inside a prison, let alone experienced conditions 'for real', and the incarceration was to prove a catalyst for the entire remainder of his life.

On his release he campaigned for better conditions and for a more active exchange of prisoners held in foreign jails. In 1756 he moved to his small estate at Cardington and turned his attention to the living conditions of the estate workers. They lived in what were little more than hovels. Howard had the shacks pulled down and replaced with proper stone-built structures, each with their own garden for growing produce. The children were given a basic education, and tenants were required to refrain from spending their energies in the local public house, and to attend divine service once a week.

In 1758 Howard again gave his marriage vows, this time to a woman of much the same age and social class. His bride, Henrietta, was also in poor health, and for her sake Howard moved with her to the edge of the New Forest, believing that the country air would be good for her. Sadly, Henrietta was to die just seven years into the marriage, leaving her husband to bring up their baby son, known as Jack.

Jack must have spent a lonely childhood, because his restless father embarked on various long tours both across Britain and in Europe (France, Germany and in particular the Netherlands). During these tours Jack was farmed out to an aunt in London, and at the age of 4 was sent off to boarding school. His father, meanwhile, continued to be afflicted by attacks of gout and ill health, but he was ever-mindful of his duties to others less well-off, and when he was made High Sheriff of Bedfordshire in 1773, he insisted on visiting the county jail because it came within his purlieu. He was deeply shocked at what he saw; it is worth remembering that jailers were not paid by the community, they were paid by the fees they charged to those who were in their custody. Corruption was endemic, with jailers charging extortionate amounts for food and water, or making money by selling alcohol, or demanding sexual favours from female miscreants – and it wasn't as if you needed to be guilty of a serious offence to find yourself locked up. People could be imprisoned for years in debtors' prisons, or held for months awaiting trial. Even those who had served their sentences, or had been acquitted, could remain incarcerated until the jailer felt that he had been sufficiently rewarded for his troubles.

It is also worth remembering that criminal trials were a farce; men (and women) could be sentenced to death after a trial which barely lasted twenty minutes. Trials did not involve a counsel for the defence. Hearsay and circumstantial evidence were often sufficient to secure a conviction. Penalties could be draconian and arguably the lucky ones were those sentenced to death, rather than enduring interminable years in truly dreadful conditions.

This was the background to a fervour which enveloped John Howard for the rest of his life. He was determined not just to find out the true state of the prisons, but also to persuade others to do something about it – and that meant persuading parliament. He needed evidence, and he needed comparisons (to show how other countries dealt with their prison populations). To that end he embarked on a series of gruelling visits, calling on virtually all the jails, houses of correction and hospitals throughout the country. He was especially alarmed at the way smallpox and typhus (known at the time as 'jail fever') were prevalent in all prisons. In cramped, fetid conditions such infections spread like wildfire, and in an age where little was known about the contagious nature of disease it did not take much of a guess to suggest that the spread of these illnesses was exacerbated by the conditions of confinement. Horwood argued that condemning a person to death by disease was not a mark of a civilised society – and nor was it necessary.

As a first stage Horwood, aided by other like-minded philanthropists, petitioned parliament to end the anomaly whereby prisoners who had been acquitted could still find themselves kept in jail simply because they could not afford to pay 'an exit fee'. He also argued that jailers should be paid a living wage out of the public purse, but this was considered a step too far and the change was not introduced into law until after Howard's lifetime.

In 1774 he was called to give evidence before the House of Commons and this was followed by a petition of gratitude from parliament for the 'humanity and zeal which have led him to visit the several gaols of this kingdom, and to communicate to the House the interesting observations he has made on that subject.' For Howard, this was merely the beginning and the final seventeen years of his life were devoted to touring prisons in Britain and Europe, looking at the good (never in Britain) the bad, and the ugly (very often in Britain). He made recommendations based on prison design, called for better living conditions, better food, segregation of prisoners based upon age and gender, religious instruction, exercise and the value of reforming the criminal mind.

He made seven major journeys between 1775 and 1790, taking in not just France Germany and Switzerland, but also Denmark, Sweden and Russia, along with

Wales and Ireland. By early 1777 he had decided that he had enough information to publish his findings and spent some months honing his report, getting the grammar and punctuation corrected, and finally going into print with his *The State of the Prisons in England and Wales, with Preliminary Observations, and an Account of some Foreign Prisons*, published later that same year.

It was an astonishing and thorough analysis of the problem of looking after the country's prison population, methodically looking at the state of the prisons throughout the kingdom. Up until then, few prisons were built for that purpose – as often as not they were poorly ventilated store rooms constructed under bridges, or old dungeons, or rat-infested basements with inadequate sanitation. Howard called for new, purpose-built, prisons with inmates segregated according to age, gender and the nature of their offences. Medical care and religious instruction were called for. He recommended that solitary confinement should be used to help the criminal come to terms with the error of his or her ways, to repent and to reform.

Some of the analysis in *The State of Prisons* still makes uncomfortable reading today. Howard describes his initial concern at visiting different prisons, writing, 'I guarded myself by smelling of vinegar, while I was in those places, and changing my apparel afterwards.' Vinegar or no vinegar, he frequently caught illnesses and indeed eventually died of a fever while visiting a prison in Kherson, in Southern Russia. His death, on 20 January 1790, was duly reported in the *London Gazette*, and a statue in his honour was erected at St Paul's Cathedral. Mind you, he would have hated such nonsense – refusing steadfastly to sit for a portrait in his lifetime, banning the raising of funds to pay for a sculpture of his likeness, and generally spurning any form of personal recognition of the hardships he so willingly endured.

He cannot have been an easy man to like – rising at three in the morning to conduct his business, visiting jails at odd hours often without prior warning so as to catch people off-guard, sometimes having to adopt an alias to gain admission, posing as a member of the medical profession or whatever. His strict religious views would mark him out nowadays as a bigot, but in his day this was simply the driving force behind all that he did. He wanted to improve the lot of mankind, and his daily routine reflected this. No matter that his son Jack was a tortured soul, never able to live up to his father's expectations, dying in a lunatic asylum in 1799. What mattered to John Howard was his belief that men were capable of being reformed, that prison should not just be about punishment, and that change was in the interests of all aspects of society. It may not have been a popular message, and at times his voice may have gone unheard, but eventually improvements were made. His personal dedication to the task in hand was remarkable: he himself calculated that he had travelled some 42,033 miles while studying prison conditions throughout Europe.

That is 42,033 miles over often dreadful roads, using indifferent transport, in all weathers, visiting places where tourists were neither expected nor catered for.

Howard had spoken out against the appalling conditions in which prisoners were kept in rotten ships moored in the Thames, especially after the outbreak of the American War of Independence meant that convicts were no longer shipped out to the American colonies to serve their punishment. His ideas on avoiding jail fever were way ahead of their time, but eventually new purpose-built prisons were constructed, with proper medical supervision and facilities for treatment. Same-sex prison quarters were introduced, and felons were eventually separated from debtors.

No wonder that in the century after his death Howard became recognised for his philanthropy and 'doing good' and the fact that today the Howard League for Penal Reform bears his name and is still instrumental in pursuing his ideals is a testament to his extraordinary vision and sense of purpose.

Josiah Spode I, 1733–1797 and Josiah Spode II, 1755–1827

Ask anyone to name the most important potter of the eighteenth century and the chances are that they would name Josiah Wedgwood. He was, of course, a great industrialist, a hugely successful marketeer – and a potter. He was the pioneer who opened a showroom in London displaying the whole range of his items, all duly priced; issued a catalogue of all his wares; was reportedly the first to offer money-back guarantees; and the first to make a Buy-One-Get-One-Free offer. But his fame tends to overshadow every other potter in the business, and that is particularly hard on a father and son who both went by the name of Josiah Spode.

No one could say that the older Josiah had been born with a silver spoon in his mouth. He had been born in 1733, the son of yet another Josiah, living in one of the small villages since absorbed into Stoke-on-Trent. He came from a line of potters, in a poorly paid industry where an adult employed as a thrower, handler or painter might be paid as little as 9 shillings a week. By the time Josiah was 6 years old, both his parents had died and, like many in the pottery industry, Josiah would have started working in a pot-shop. At 16 he gained an apprenticeship with Thomas Whieldon. His pay (according to Whieldon's records): 'two shillings and three pence a week, or if he deserves it, two shillings and sixpence.' Josiah Wedgwood became a partner of Whieldon in 1754 and would have worked alongside Spode. At an early stage, the link between the Spode and Wedgwood families was established, and the two Josiah's became close friends, despite any commercial rivalry which later developed. Spode married a girl called Ellen Finley in 1754, and their eldest son, also named Josiah, was born the following year. Seven other children followed.

The pottery industry was undergoing a revolution, with new materials, new colours and new designs. Fine salt-glazed stoneware with delicate ornamentation vied for popularity with white earthenware of the highest quality. It was a period when Wedgwood was about to launch creamware, later known as Queen's Ware after Queen Charlotte ordered a complete dinner service of this distinctive material in 1765. Other potters were also experimenting, and the new rich elite – the successful traders and entrepreneurs who made up an emerging middle class – snapped up anything new and fashionable. They wanted a change from platters made from wood or pewter and, in order to replace them, they bought fine dinner services, tea services and so on in large quantities.

Spode was keen to acquire his own premises and to establish himself as a master potter. To put the time-line in perspective, Josiah Wedgwood, who was three years his senior, had started his business as a master potter in 1759. By 1762 Spode appears to have taken over the management of the Stoke factory belonging to William Banks, and for a time rented premises belonging to other master potters. He had a number of financial backers throughout the 1770s, including a local solicitor called William Tomlinson who went into partnership with him between 1767 and 1774. In 1772 he had acquired premises of his own, at Shelton, having entered into a partnership for that purpose with Thomas Mountford.

In 1776 he was able to acquire the old William Banks factory outright. There he produced creamware, often with blue decoration, and a fine white-glazed earthenware. He also produced blackware and experimented with printing black transfers. The business quickly took off, but it did not stop Spode experimenting with new finishes and designs. Sometime between 1781 and 1784 he came up with blue underglaze transfer printing, and in around 1790 he introduced a range of pottery decorated with the willow pattern – one of the most popular and long-lasting designs of all time. In the late 1780s he developed a formula for making a form of soft paste porcelain called bone china, which completely transformed the English market. The public could not get enough of the white, translucent material, and bone china – so-called because of the high content of bone ash used in its manufacturing process – became fashionable everywhere.

Aware that in 1765 Wedgwood had opened showroom premises in Charles Street, Mayfair to cater to the growing market for high-class consumer-goods in London, Spode hankered after his own London premises. The opportunity came when his eldest son, Josiah II, married Elizabeth Barker in 1775 and was given the job of developing the London connection from premises at Fore Street in Cripplegate. To this end, father entered into a partnership with his friend William Copeland. The younger Spode had the marketing skills to ensure that the venture was a business triumph. He became a Liveryman of the Spectacle Makers Company (there was no London guild for potters) and was made a Freeman of the City in 1778. Sadly, Josiah II's wife died in 1782, having had five children in as many years.

These included Josiah III, who later went on to become the father of Josiah IV. In this way the Spode dynasty was ensured well into the next century. Josiah II stayed in London for most of his time, moving the centre of operations to larger premises and eventually settling on much more prestigious (rented) premises in Portugal Street, Lincoln's Inn Fields. These were the premises of the old Theatre Royal where, years before, John Gay had put on The Beggar's Opera, and the premises are shown in the engraving at the end of this chapter.

Two years later, in 1797, Josiah I died leaving his share in the business to Josiah II. A man of many parts – a keen flautist, a politician, a shrewd businessman and a member of the local yeomanry – Josiah II capitalised on the reduction in tax levels on imported tea by promoting the sale of tea services. He also ensured that his firm's bone china was on the tables of all the finest households, as well as developing a thriving export market.

By 1802 he was able to buy outright the premises in Portugal Street along with the adjoining residential properties, thus ensuring room for expansion. Josiah II was granted a coat of arms in 1804, and in 1806 was honoured by a visit from the Prince of Wales, resulting in Spode being given the title of 'Potter and English Porcelain Manufacturer to H.R.H. Prince of Wales'. The bone china was known generally as 'Stoke china', and it was augmented with a range of earthenware manufactured to a new and improved recipe, which he called 'Stone china'. This had the advantage of being much stronger and more resistant to damage. In general, the stone china wares were richly decorated in the Chinese style.

The wares produced in the Stoke factory became increasingly decorated in more elaborate ways: new gilding and enamelling techniques were employed along with lustre decoration. What was known as bat-printing enabled transfers to be applied, especially showing topographical scenes. In 1816 the company brought out its 'Italian' pattern, which quickly became an established favourite for many years. Other products were enhanced by gilded borders to give a really opulent feel to the product. In 1805 Henry Daniel, one of the foremost decorators of porcelain in the country, opened a branch inside the Spode premises, dedicated to decorating Spode merchandise.

In 1822 Josiah introduced feldspar to the manufacturing process. It revolutionised production, making it more reliable and giving it an attractive finish by acting as a flux which was used both in the clay body and in the glaze applied to it. Felspar has a high alumina and silica content, and its introduction helped felspar ware become the forerunner of all modern bone china. In turn it led to the Spode factory becoming the largest manufacturer of bone china worldwide.

Josiah II saw the value and importance of harnessing steam power to many aspects of the production, leading in turn to Spode forming a partnership with a number of other potters to acquire an interest in a newly opened colliery at Fenton Park.

Another joint venture involved the acquisition of quarry premises at Carloggas in Cornwall, where china clay was extracted. He also acquired land at Penkhull, in the vicinity of the Stoke pot-works and built himself a fine mansion called The Mount, set in 17 acres of rolling parkland.

Back in London, the retail business was handed over to William, son of Josiah II, in 1805. For the next six years William operated the business under the Spode name but in partnership with William Copeland; eventually Copeland took over the business and traded as Spode & Copeland.

Josiah Spode died on 16 July 1827 in Stoke-on-Trent, by which time he was pre-eminent in his field. The company continued under the guise of various different names until it went into administration in 2008 and was subsequently acquired by Portmeirion.

Father and son deserve to be remembered for helping to change the dining habits of the nation – a meal served in 1837 was presented in a very different way to one presented a century earlier. This was as true for the wealthy aristocrat dining on bone china as it was to the poorest of workmen eating off a piece of willow-pattern earthenware. Spode? Wedgwood? Take your pick, even if only one is still a household name.

An engraving from 1811 showing the Spode premises, previously the Theatre Royal, in Portugal Street, Lincoln's Inn Fields.

Chapter 9

Washday Blues and the Green,
Green Grass of Home

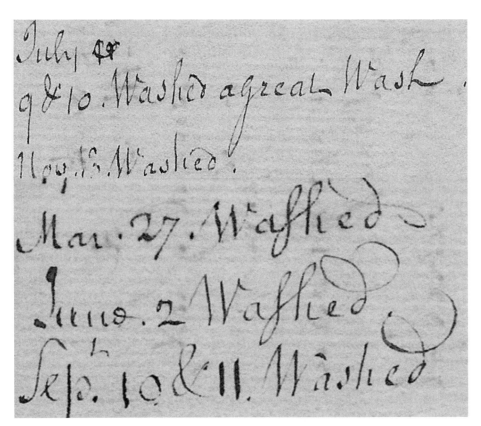

One for the diary: 'Wash'd a great wash' – i.e. did the laundry.

Edward Beetham, c. 1744–c. 1808

It was always a major operation washing all the sheets, shirts and other linen items in the early Georgian era. The poor servant charged with the laundry had to start the day before, gathering all the wood needed to light a fire sufficient to heat the 20 gallons or so of water in the copper bowl to boiling point, and to maintain it at that temperature for at least a quarter of an hour. The servant would also need to fetch and carry another 10 gallons or so of water for rinsing. Heavily soiled garments would be left to soak overnight. Early on the morning of the great wash, the laundress would then light her fire, and busily stir the garments and sheets, taking them out to rub and scrub each one individually. Another worker had the heavy job of wielding a cumbersome paddle back and forth, agitating the water and hopefully loosening the dirt. Some laundresses used a metal cone on a wooden handle – generally called 'possers' in England, or plungers in the United States. Other names for the stirring instrument were dollies, 'possing-sticks', or 'poshers'.

Water was not the only ingredient – the laundress would also add leys to get rid of stains. Traditionally the leys would be made from ash from the hearth, soaked in water and allowed to percolate down through a filter by packing straw into a barrel in which holes had been drilled in the bottom. This alkaline mix was good for grease spots, but other additives would also be used, such as milk (believed to be the answer for fruit stains) and chalk or brick dust. To this might be added a small amount of urine – another useful means of bleaching out stains. Each laundress would have her own magic formula, some using alcohol, others vinegar, and others lemon juice to remove stains, in an attempt to restore sheets and garments alike to their former glory. If you had sufficient leys you did not need soap, but as one visitor to the capital remarked in 1719:

> *At London, and in all other Parts of the Country where they do not burn Wood, they do not make Ley. All their Linnen, coarse and fine, is wash'd with Soap. When you are in a Place where the Linnen can be rinc'd in any large Water, the Stink of the black Soap is almost all clear'd away.*

The black soap mentioned by the writer, a Mr Misson, in his *Memoirs and Observations in his Travels over England* was made by mixing unslaked lime with potash, and boiling it for many hours. Various extra ingredients including oil could also be added. White soap could be obtained by adding quantities of salt to the mixture, while recipes abounded for making your washing fragrant by adding crushed rose petals to the foul-smelling concoction.

After hours of toil, the items would then be rinsed thoroughly before being hung out to dry on fences and hedges. First, though, the material had to be fed through a mangle, or, if funds did not run to such equipment, had to be wrung out by the simple expedient of two servants twisting and stretching the material, forcing out the excess water.

Coloureds would be treated separately, using tepid or cold water. Colour could be restored, somewhat laboriously, by boiling-up powdered terracotta (e.g. from broken flower pots) with birch leaves, adding a couple of ox galls, and then shredding up rags of the desired colour. Boil it all up, leave it for a fortnight for the colour to be extracted from the cut rag and wash your faded garment in the mixture. It would surely restore it to its former glory.... Meanwhile stains on satins and damask could be removed by rubbing the affected areas with 'crumbs from a threepenny loaf, two days old, mixed with a quarter of an ounce of powder-blue'.

Anything needing to be starched would be soaked separately in the water which the cook had saved and which had previously been used for cooking potatoes or rice. Small wonder that the servants loathed the approach of laundry day, and often postponed it so that a big wash only took place four or five times a year. And imagine the chaos if it came on to rain during the drying process – damp washing must have been draped around spare rooms, over the backs of chairs, in front of the roaring fire – anywhere that space permitted.

Into this far-from-halcyon scene came a man who was determined to put an end to the miseries of the laundry. He didn't claim to have invented the washing machine – but he bought out patents granted to others, and set about introducing the public to the wonders of the washing mill. He was a marketeer, and he knew a good idea when he saw one.

His name was Edward Beetham and he was something of an actor-cum-entrepreneur. He had been named Edward Betham after being born near Penrith in Cumbria in 1744, and was the eldest of three children. Little is known of his early years but when he was around 30 he fell for the charms of someone called Isabella Robinson, a girl some ten years his junior. More to the point, she came from a Roman Catholic family, and the Betham family strongly disapproved. The couple eloped in 1764 and, to spare the family any embarrassment, added an 'e' to their name. Mr and Mrs Beetham then travelled south to seek employment on the London stage, particularly at the Haymarket and at Sadler's Wells. Edward turned his hand to inventing the first safety curtain for theatres – a much-needed invention given that naked flames were used in footlights. But Edward did not have the money to take out a patent for his idea. Nevertheless, the couple prospered and Isabella took to cutting out silhouettes, painting them on to card and later onto glass and plaster. She was extraordinarily talented, operating initially from their premises in Coe Lane, Clerkenwell. In time she became the foremost silhouettist of the time. She also bore Edward six children.

In 1787, Edward Beetham went into partnership with Thomas Todd, who had just been granted a patent for a 'machine for the washing and ironing of linen, woollen and cotton stuffs, silks, carpets, and every other woven or knit fabric.' In those days it was not necessary to have made such a machine in order to get a patent, merely to think of the idea. It looks as though the practical steps were taken by Edward. There is also a reference to a patent taken out by a Mr James Wood of Kent Road, which Wood sold to Edward in 1790. By then the couple had moved to a building at 27 The Strand, where Edward ran a shop and warehouse downstairs, while Isabella operated her portrait studio upstairs.

By 1791 Edward was posting advertisements in the London newspapers:

> MR. BEETHAM's KEW PATENT PORTABLE WASHING MILL, is so universally useful and economical, that it deserves the serious attention of the public in general.
>
> 1st. It renders the linen whiter and cleaner than it can be made by any other method, and will wash a Bank Bill without injuring it.
>
> 2d. It will wash more in one hour than Ten women or any other Two machines can in the same time.
>
> 3dly. It is so saving that for Five shillings it will wash as much as will cost One Guinea in the common mode.

The same advertisement announced that: 'N.B. One Thousand and Twenty were Sold between the 1st of May 1790 and the 1st of May 1791.' Another advertisement, appearing in *The Times*, explained that Beetham had developed a machine 'for washing linen which will, in an equal space of time, wash as much linen as six or eight of the ablest washerwomen, without the use of lees [lye], and with only one third of the fire and soap.' In other words, it was established early on that the key advantages were that it saved on labour, it was more economical, it used less soap, it reduced the amount of firewood which had to be collected, and so on.

The wringing machine was separate and cost 1 guinea, and the washing machine itself came in various different sizes. In time there was even one designed for use on naval ships.

Edward Beetham was a colourful and energetic salesman, and inevitably others soon came to the market offering different variations on a theme. Some splendid 'knocking copy' followed, rubbishing the competition and explaining why the Beetham Washing Mill was a cut above the opposition. Some users apparently felt that rival machines damaged the linen, and one of Beetham's advertisements quickly proclaimed that with his machine, 'the common objection to machines, that they destroy the linen is, in the present invention, totally removed ... entirely free from friction ... works by pressure only.'

Beetham also enlisted the support of the governors of St James Workhouse, Clerkenwell, in London, who happily supplied a commendation to the effect that using one of Beetham's machines they had washed:

> between the hours of nine in the morning and nine at night, in a common Mill of six guineas value ... consuming only nine and a half pounds of soap and a pound of pearl ashes wrung in a common wringer, value 1 guinea ...

350 shirts and shifts, each worn a week
64 aprons, ditto
36 handkerchiefs
10 gowns
10 frocks
2 long table cloths
48 sheets, worn a month
caps and other small things…

To provide the labour-saving comparison, the commendation went on to say that washing the same quantity by hand always took seven women two days.

As he prospered, his family entertained widely, and the family records refer to poets, writers and artists being entertained at their house, along with Captain William Bligh (he of the Bounty fame). Edward Beetham experimented with a number of other inventions, including what he called 'a chiropedal car'. This, so he stated, could carry 'two persons up or down a hill, and without horses, six miles an hour, is the most useful, pleasant, economical, and expeditious mode of Travelling that can possibly be adopted.' Apparently this admirable invention was 'to be seen for One Shilling each Person … at Beetham's repositories, Nos. 26 and 27 Fleet Street.'

Beetham published a variety of pamphlets and books including Stackhouse's *History of the Bible* in 1787. As well as his washing mill, he sold mangles and butter churns, and amazed the public with a 'scientific' demonstration of how washing with soap alone compared with washing with a combination of soap and soda.

He died on 18 February 1809 at 27 Fleet Street, and was buried at old St Pancras Church. It was not of course the end of the story: the first of his machines had reached the United States in 1791, although the first washing machine to be patented in the US was made by Nathaniel Briggs. Later years saw the patenting of the built-in wringer, while rivals Coates and Hancock offered a 'money-back guarantee if not completely satisfied within one month of purchase'. They made a great point of stressing that their machines were far gentler on clothes and that they obviated the need for hand-scrubbing cuffs and collars. In their words: 'the finest muslins can be washed more safely than can possibly be done by hand.'

Some years later came the scrub-board, consisting of two carved wood planks which were moved by means of a lever, causing the clothes to be rubbed over each other. Although this device was invented in around 1797, it was first patented in the US in 1846. Then there was the first washing machine using a rotating drum which had been patented by Henry Sidgier in 1782. Variations using a paddle as well as a revolving drum were patented in 1851, and a reverse action drum was patented in America in 1858 by Hamilton Smith. And the rest, as they say, is history….

Edwin Beard Budding, 1796–1846

Few men can have had a greater impact on the way we spend our spare time, or on English gardens and gardening, than Edwin Beard Budding – and yet his is hardly a household name, even in Gloucestershire where he was born in 1796.

His father was a farmer called Charles Brain Budding and his mother, Mary Beard, may well have been a servant girl. There is no record of a marriage, but he appears to have been brought up with a number of siblings and half-siblings. His education, in a remote farming community, would have been rudimentary if not non-existent, but he was obviously a practical person who enjoyed problem solving. In all likelihood he started work as a carpenter, but it is believed that he drifted into working on the fringes of the local weaving industry, which was by then in decline. In March 1821 Edwin married Elizabeth Chew, a woman who, at 28, was probably two or three years his senior. They went on to have three children.

At some point in time, Budding gained the acquaintance of John Ferrabee, a man who owned several textile mills. In 1827 he had taken over the Phoenix Mill at Thrupp, near Stroud, and then developed those premises as an ironworks, manufacturing castings and parts needed for his textile mills. He also made farm instruments and waterwheels. Budd worked with him, but not on an exclusive basis since he is also believed to have worked with another iron master, a man called John Lewis. Back in 1815, Lewis had come up with an idea for a cutting machine to be used in the textile industry. A helical blade mounted on a bench revolved, and as it turned the blade moved across the cloth, neatly decapitating any long threads and leaving the cloth with a uniform, even, nap. Up until then, the process involved skilled craftsmen using hand shears.

The story goes that Budding was observing the napping machine in use just as men arrived with scythes to cut the meadow outside. Budding was convinced that with a simple adaptation, the machine could be used as a grass mower. It was not the first idea he had had for an invention. Some time after 1825 he came up with the idea for a 'Pepper Box' pistol, some ten years earlier than the one invented by Samuel Colt and patented in 1836. By some accounts, the Budding pistol was not only earlier, but also had practical advantages over its American rival.

Budding knew that he did not have the money, or knowledge, to take matters further on his own with the development of his grass-cutting machine, so he enlisted the help of Ferrabee. The two agreed to go into partnership, sharing profits once Ferrabee had recovered his out-of-pocket costs in developing the machine, and obtaining the requisite patent. The story that the pair of them experimented at night, so as not to alarm the locals or raise suspicion, may be apocryphal, but over a short period of time the two of them were able to adapt the helical blade so that it operated with a pair of wheels, geared to allow for easy movement. The cutting width was only 19in, and the grass was 'guillotined' against a rigid bar, before being thrown forward ahead of the moving machine. A simple form of basket was used to collect the clippings. Motive power came from an adult pushing the machine forward and slightly downwards. A front roller, without gearing, rotated freely and could be set at different levels to allow for adjustments to be made to the height of the cut.

By means of patent number 6081, dated 31 August 1830, the pair were granted a patent for their cast-iron machine, which by then had been adapted so that there was a pulling bar at the front, thereby making it a two-man operation. In the application, Budding was described as 'a machinist' from Thrupp in Gloucestershire.

He extolled the advantages of the grass cutter by pointing out that:

> *Grass growing in the shade, too weak to stand against a scythe to be cut, may be cut by my machine as closely as required, and the eye will never be offended by those circular scars, inequalities, and bare places, so commonly made by the best mowers with the scythe, and which continue visible for several days.*

Budding further claimed that 'Country gentlemen may find, in using my machine themselves, an amusing, useful, and healthy exercise'. Intriguingly the advertisements showed a gentleman, resplendent in top hat and tails, gently pushing his Budding machine as if it was as light as a feather.

Different sizes of models emerged, one with a 16in blade and the other of 21in. The mowers were promoted as being for 'the purpose of cropping or shearing the vegetable surface of Lawns, Grass-plats and Pleasure Grounds', and initial sales concentrated on owners of larger grassed areas, such as Regent's Park Zoological Gardens. In time it transformed meadows into lawns. No longer was a team of labourers required to assemble at dawn (while the grass was sufficiently dew-laden to be cut by scythe). No longer would Londoners see the sunrise greeted by a whole army of men, wheeling and turning, slicing through the meadow of Hyde Park. Instead, they could see two men operating as a mowing team, one pushing and the other pulling, and leaving behind a neatly rolled carpet of green.

John Ferrabee quickly realised that his connections in the manufacturing trades were not sufficient to cope with the new grass cutters. In 1832 he approached Ransomes, Sims, and Jeffries of Ipswich, well-established manufacturers of agricultural machinery such as plough-shares, and agreed that they could produce the machines under licence. Over 1,000 of the machines were sold in the first ten years, with Ransome's advertising that: 'The machine is so easy to manage, that persons unpractised in the art of Mowing, may cut the Grass on Lawns, and Bowling Greens with ease.'

The instructions for use were delightfully straightforward: '...take hold of the handles, as in driving a barrow, ...push the machine steadily forward along the greensward, without lifting the handles, but rather exerting a moderate pressure downwards...'

Budding then turned his hand to various other inventions and he is credited with having come up with the idea of an adjustable spanner (cutting out the need for wedges to hold the spanner head in position). This was patented in 1843 and the spanners were being made by John Ferrabee at the Phoenix Ironworks from that year onwards. He also came up with a cutting machine which could be used on a variety of materials, such as leather, and also on root vegetables and sugar cane. The patent for this was granted jointly to Budding and to Francis, second Earl of Ducie and Richard Clyburn, in 1840.

By then Budding had moved to Dursley to take up an appointment as manager of the card-making and wire-pulling factory owned by George Lister. In 1843 he took out a patent for a device which made the carding more efficient by the 'covering of cylinders with card clothing under tension and arranging for it to be wound helically.' Sadly, Edward Beard Budding suffered a stroke, causing paralysis, and he died in 1846, before the full impact of his invention of the lawn mower had become evident. By then garden designers had written enthusiastically about his machine to end the tyranny of scythe-operators – and sheep. A thousand sales became 5,000, and then by the middle of the nineteenth century, sales had rocketed into the tens of thousands. It may have taken time for the invention to launch the craze for owning your own plot of grass – but it became a craze which reached down to the most humble of homes. Eventually, villas with front and back gardens the size of a pocket handkerchief were put to turf, and even today 1 million homes are believed to have their own piece of lawn. That is a million households where a weekly cutting of the grass, throughout the growing season, is a ritual enjoyed and endured by many. And it all dates back to Mr Budding...

Could we have had Wembley Stadium if we needed a herd of sheep or fallow deer to munch the grass short enough to enable sportsmen to perform on it? Without Budding would we be visiting Lords to see cricket played in the long grass? Would crown green bowlers, golfers and tennis players at Wimbledon have been able to hone their skills if they first had to clear sheep from the pitches, greens and courts which nowadays are so immaculately trimmed? Probably not. Budding enabled a lot of things to happen – here was a man who could genuinely say that he changed the world. Not many can claim that much – and yet still be generally unknown and invisible. He is the ultimate forgotten hero of the Georgian era.

Right and below: On the right, an advertisement for Beetham's washing machine and below, a picture showing that anyone pushing a Budding lawn-mower should definitely wear a top hat at all times.

Conclusion

So, what is the conclusion to be drawn from this list of disparate movers and shakers of the Georgian era? The contributions of 'key' individuals such as Boulton and Wedgwood have been deliberately omitted, along with household names like Chippendale, Hepplewhite and Sheraton. They did their bit and everyone knows about them. Capability Brown doesn't get a look-in for the same reason – because a spotlight on the famous merely blinds us to the contribution of others. For that reason, there is no Robert Adam, no Beau Brummel, no Robert Stephenson. Above all, by concentrating on the already well known, we lose sight of the fact that many of the changes were made slowly in stages. It was not so much an industrial revolution as an industrial evolution.

Sometimes fame sticks to the innovator – in modern parlance, first-mover advantage – but in practice it usually attaches itself to he who shouts loudest (and yes, Mr Arkwright, if the cap fits, wear it). Others, such as James Watt, are famous for improving what had already been invented by others.

Some of the choices may seem out of place, but think for a moment of today's social media and the perceived importance of 'influencers', often followed by millions. On that basis, Dr Gill deserves his place in the pantheon of greatness, because millions of people across the world followed his teachings. And because of that, he helped change our world. Some of those included were unaware of the commercial significance of their contribution. Some grew rich. Some may have very consciously developed their ideas for the public good, especially those who were linked to groups such as the Lunar Society, where members met to discuss the direction in which they wanted to take their inventions and discoveries. Others made discoveries by accident and left it to others to realise the commercial implications. Money was not necessarily a consideration; Trevithick or Clarkson may not at first sight have had a lot in common, but for both men it was sufficient that their efforts improved the world around them, making life easier for others. In some cases, such as Howard or Gill, they had a sense of purpose bordering on the obsessive; others seemed to have the attention spell of a gnat, and flitted from project to project.

By and large, the people mentioned in this book played a vital part in how the world took shape in the eighteenth century. It was a century marked by a growing consumerism, the emergence of an affluent middle class, greater mobility and an awareness of Britain's place in the world. The test has been: did this person's life make a change which we can still detect in today's world? Has that contribution been fairly recognised? Of course, there are hundreds of others who could have been included. Their omission does not mean that they were unimportant, simply that space is insufficient to record their contributions. The eighteenth century was a period of immense change, and that change was not down to the few, but to the many.

Above all, the men featured in the book show three things. The first, of course, is that they were exclusively male. No woman makes it into the list because this was an era dominated by men. As *Trailblazing Women of the Georgian Era* demonstrates, there were women who made a difference, but their achievements have not been ranked alongside the giants of the Industrial Revolution – not least because they were not allowed to. Any credit for ideas and discoveries would have been taken by their male counterparts. The education of women, and the role they were expected to play in society, did not lend itself to encourage women to make waves, either in the Arts or in the Sciences. Secondly, the list shows the importance of a Nonconformist background to an inquisitive mind, with many of the people featured here being Dissenters. The final point is that the people featured have been treated shabbily by history and they have been denied the fame which their efforts justified. Our present world is obsessed with fame – but at least it should be doled out in a fair and consistent manner. This book is intended to help redress the imbalance.

Trevithick's railroad 'Catch-me-who-can', exhibited at Euston, 1809.

Bibliography

Altick, Richard Dani: *Shows Of London*. The Belknap Press (Harvard University Press) United States, (1978).

Babbage, Charles: *Passages from the Life of a Philosopher*, London, (1864).

Barrie, David: *Sextant: A Voyage Guided by the Stars and the Men Who Mapped the World's Oceans*. William Collins, 2014

Bradbury, Frederick: *History of Old Sheffield Plate*. Macmillan & Co 1912

Bruyns, W F J Mörzer: *Sextants at Greenwich: A Catalogue of the Mariner's Quadrants, etc…* Oxford University Press, 2009

Burney, (afterwards, D'Arblay) Frances: *Diary and Letters of Madame D'Arblay*, ed. Austin Dobson, 1904

Busby, Thomas: *Concert Room and Orchestra Anecdotes*. London, (1805).

Cantrell, John, and Cookson, Gillian: *Henry Maudslay and the Pioneers of the Machine*. NPI Media Group, London, 2002.

Clements, Paul: *Marc Isambard Brunel*. Phillimore & Co. Ltd., Bognor Regis, 2008

Darwin, Charles: *On the Origin of Species by Means of Natural Selection, (or the Preservation of Favoured Races in the Struggle for Life)*. John Murray, London, 1859.

Darwin, Charles: *The Variation of Animals and Plants under Domestication*. John Murray, London, 1868

Dawson, Frank: *John Wilkinson, King of the Ironmasters*. The History Press, Stroud, 2012.

Gill, John: *Exposition of the Old and New Testaments* London, 1746-66. See https://www.biblestudytools.com/commentaries/gills-exposition-of-the-bible/genesis for the e-version.

Greater London Council: *John Joseph Merlin – the Ingenious Mechanick*, London, (1985).

Hayden, Arthur: *Spode & his successors*. Cassell & Co, London, 1925.

Hill, Draper: *Mr. Gillray: The caricaturist* Phaidon Press, New York, 1965.

Howard, John: *The State of the Prisons in England and Wales: With Preliminary Observations*. William Eyres, London, 1777. Also available in electronic format.

Johnson, Mary: *Madam Johnson's Present: Or, Every Young Woman's Companion in Useful and Universal Knowledge*. J Williams, Dublin circa 1770. Also available in electronic format.

King-Hele, Desmond: *Erasmus Darwin – A Life of Unequalled Achievement*. Giles de la Mare Publishers Ltd, London, 1999

La Roche, Sophie von: *Sophie in England*, a translation of the passages on England in the *Journal of a Journey through Holland and England* (1788), trans. Clare Williams. London: Jonathan Cape, (1933).

Lane, Joan: *Apprenticeship In England, 1600–1914*. UCL Press, London, 1996.

Marshall, William: *Rural Economy of the Midland Counties including the Management of livestock in Leicestershire and its environs*. Vols 1 and 2. London, 1790. Also available in electronic format.

Monk, John: *General View of the Agriculture of the County of Leicester with observations on their means of improvement*. Vinton & Company, Ltd., London 1909.

Prothero, R.E. [later Lord Ernle], *English Farming Past and Present*. 6th edition by G.E. Fussell and O.R. McGregor, (1961).

Repton, Humphry: *Sketches and Hints on Landscape Gardening*. W Bulmer & Co, London, 1794. Also available in electronic format.

Repton, Humphry: *Observations on the Theory and Practice of Landscape Gardening*. J. Taylor, Architectural Library, London, 1803. Also available in digital format

Repton, Humphry: *Fragments on the Theory and Practice of Landscape Gardening* J. Taylor, Architectural Library, London, 1816. Also available in electronic format.

Rippon, John: *A brief memoir of the life and writings of the late Rev. John Gill, D.D.* London 1838.

Rolt, LTC: *The Cornish Giant: The Story of Richard Trevithick, Father of the Steam Locomotive* Lutterworth Press 1960

Rolt, LTC: *George and Robert Stephenson: The Railway Revolution*. Longmans 1960

Rolt, LTC: *Thomas Newcomen: The Prehistory of the Steam Engine*. David & Charles, 1968

Stalker, John, and Parker, George: *A treatise of japaning and varnishing*. Oxford, 1688

Stanley, Pat: *Robert Bakewell and the Longhorn Breed of Cattle*. Farming Press Books, Ipswich, (1995).

Stuart, James: *The Antiquities of Athens*. Printed by J. Haberkorn, London 1762. Also available in electronic format.

Walling, Philip: *Counting Sheep: A Celebration of the Pastoral Heritage of Britain*. Profile Books, London, 2014.

Wilson, James: *The evolution of British cattle and the fashioning of breeds*. Vinton & Company, Ltd., London 1909.

Websites:
'Old and interesting' at: http://www.oldandinteresting.com/edward-beetham-
    biography.aspx
'Famous scientists' at: https://www.famousscientists.org/john-michell/
'Grace's Guide to British Industrial History' at: https://www.gracesguide.co.uk/
'James Gillray, caricaturist' at: http://www.james-gillray.org/bio1.html

Image Accreditation

Text Images

Page 1, Image 1. Newcomen's fire-powered engine, by H. Beighton, 1717. Copyright Science Museum, shown under Creative Commons 4.00.

Page 20, Image 2. Diagram of the tunnelling shield used to construct the Thames Tunnel, London. Contemporary image (19th century), probably from the *Illustrated London News*. In public domain, Wikimedia Commons.

Page 21, Image 3. Trade token issued in 1787, shown courtesy of Dalton and Hamer's *'The Provincial Token Coinage of the 18th Century'*.

Page 33, Image 4. Lombe's silk-mill, 1793. In public domain.

Page 34, Image 5. William Bloye's statue of Boulton, Watt and Murdoch, photographed by Osoom at English Wikipedia. GNU Free Documentation License, Version 1.2.

Page 46, Image 6. Erasmus Darwin – polychrome wax with paint, mounted on painted glass. Artist unknown. Shown courtesy of the Philadelphia Museum of Art.

Page 47, Image 7. Baskerville sample typeface from 1757.

Page 61, Image 8. Watch made of pinchbeck, French, 1790-1800, artist unknown. Philadelphia Museum of Art.

Page 62, Image 9. A Dishley ram and ewe. Coloured stipple engraving by Neele. Credit: Wellcome Collection. CC BY.

Page 75, Image 10. Humphry Repton trade card. In public domain.

Page 76, Image 11. Michell's torsion balance. In public domain.

Page 87, Image 12a and 12b. Above: John Bird's mural quadrant, Museum of the History of Science, Oxford, per Wikimedia. Below: A John Bird sextant, copyright National Maritime Museum.

Page 88, Image 13. Astley's system of equestrian training. From Philip Astley's *The Modern Riding Master; Or, A Key to the Knowledge of the Horse and Horsemanship*, 1804. In public domain.

Page 117, Image 14. Drawing of the Temple of the Winds by James Stuart. In public domain.

Page 118, Image 15. Diagram of the *Brookes*. In public domain.

Page 134, Image 16. South View of the Theatre Royal in Portugal Street, Lincoln's Inn Fields ('now the Salopian China Warehouse') engraved by William Wise after George Shepherd. Yale Center for British Art, Paul Mellon Collection, Accession Number B1977.14.18554.

Page 135, Image 17. Diary entry for laundry ('washed a great wash') by Richard Hall. Author's own collection.

Page 143, Image 18a. Advertisement for Beetham's Royal Patent Washing Machine. In public domain.

Page 143, Image 18b. A Budding lawnmower in use. In public domain.

Page 145, Image 19. Richard Trevithick's Railroad, Euston Square, 1809, by Thomas Rowlandson. In public domain.

Plates
Plate 1a. Model of a double action beam engine by H W Fricke, 1840. Rijkmuseum.

Plate 1b. A peep at the gaslights in Pall Mall, by Thomas Rowlandson, 1809. In public domain, via Wikimedia.

Plate 2. John Joseph Merlin painted by Thomas Gainsborough in 1781. Image courtesy of American Federation of Arts.

Plate 3a. *Comforts of Bath – Gouty Gourmands at Dinner* by Thomas Rowlandson. Yale Center for British Art.

Plate 3b. *Barbarities in the West Indies*, by James Gillray. Shown courtesy of the Lewis Walpole Library, Yale University.

Plate 4 Marc Isambard Brunel by James Northcote, 1812. National Portrait Gallery NP978.

Plate 5a. *Anti-Saccharrites, or John Bull and his family leaving off the use of sugar*, by James Gillray. Shown courtesy of the Lewis Walpole Library, Yale University.

Plate 5b. *The Plumb Pudding in Danger* by James Gillray, 1805. Metropolitan Museum of Art.

Plate 6a. Spode tray, circa 1800. Metropolitan Museum of Art.

Plate 6b. Spode creamer, 1805. Philadelphia Museum of Art.

Plate 7. Joseph Wright of Derby, self-portrait. Yale Center for British Art.

Plate 8. *A Philosopher Giving that Lecture on the Orrery, in which a Lamp is put in place of the Sun* or *The Orrery* by Joseph Wright, c. 1766. Derby City Art Gallery. In public domain.

Plate 9a. Bas-relief portrait of James Stuart from the Wedgwood Museum, via Wikimedia. In public domain.

Plate 9b. Bust of John Howard over Shrewsbury Prison. By R J Higginson – Own work by uploader, of 3D object on permanent display as architectural feature, CC BY-SA 3.0, https://commons.wikimedia.org/w/index.php?curid=5814993.

Plate 10. Erasmus Darwin. Colour mezzotint by J. R. Smith, 1797, after J. Wright. Credit: Wellcome Collection. CC BY.

Plate 11. Lord Granville Leveson-Gower, later first Earl Granville by Sir Thomas Lawrence, c. 1804. Yale Centre for British Art, Paul Mellon Collection. B1981.25.736.

Plate 12. Elizabeth Farren (later, Countess of Derby) by Sir Thomas Lawrence, 1790. Metropolitan Museum of Art 50.135.5.

Plate 13. Lady Maria Conyngham by Sir Thomas Lawrence, 1824. Metropolitan Museum of Art, Accession Number 55.89.

Plate 14a. *A View of Murton Colliery near Seaham, County Durham* by John Wilson Carmichael, 1843.

Plate 14b. Engraving showing elevation, plan and engines of a paddle steamer. Credit: Wellcome Collection. CC BY.

Plate 15. Astley's Amphitheatre, 1804, in a sketch by Thomas Rowlandson. Houghton Library. In public domain.

Plate 16a. *Going it by steam* by Robert Seymour, 1828. Philadelphia Museum of Art, accession number 1963-148-77.

Plate 16b. *March of Intellect* by William Heath, 1828. Lewis Walpole Library, Yale University, lwlpr13151.

Index